As a ceramicist, I resonate with the way in which *Clay in the Potter's Hands* links the transformative process of working in clay to the transformation that can take place in the human soul. As a ceramics instructor myself, I am grateful how this book supplies those studying ceramics with helpful technical information to improve their studio practice, while also inextricably linking it to the ancient and Biblical history of clay. This revised and expanded edition of Glyer's well-loved work fits in so well with the other fine Square Halo titles for thinking about issues of art and faith, and is ideal for the maker seeking to expand their studio and spiritual practice.

—ALLISON LUCE artist

Never has the most careful Old Testament scholar explained Isaiah's image of the potter and the clay (Isa. 45:9) better than Diana Glyer in *Clay in the Potter's Hands.* Never again will I look at a clay pot in the same ordinary way. Neither will you. Read it slowly, devotionally, one chapter a day. Think on each chapter, pray over it, and find yourself molded, changed, enlightened, and encouraged.

—JOEL HECK Interim President of Concordia Lutheran Seminary, Edmonton, and the author of *No Ordinary People: Twenty-One Friendships of C. S. Lewis*

Rarely does one encounter a writer who seizes a powerful metaphor, digs deeply into its heart, and allows it to shape and inform not only her prose but her life. In *Clay in the Potter's Hands,* Diana Glyer has done just that. Here, we gently move from observer to participant and from casual knowledge to redeeming wisdom. Each step of this shaping process is filled with meaning and each meditative moment is touched with the eternal hand of the Master Potter. Diana Glyer invites her readers into the real potter's studio.

—SCOTT B. KEY Professor Emeritus at California Baptist University and co-director of the C.S. Lewis Study Center

In her book, Diana Glyer provides vivid and captivating imagery that brings delight in being mere clay in the hands of our mighty Creator. Inspiring questions accompany each chapter, culminating in prayers that lead the reader to humble awe and gratitude for being chosen and crafted into the image of God by the Potter's own hand.

—**DOUG GREENMAN** pastor of Echo Church

I've read dozens of devotional books. Okay, well, I've started dozens of them, but with very few exceptions they usually leave me uninspired. But Diana Glyer has managed the nearly impossible: to sound the deep places of the heart with healing, humor, wisdom, and grace. I do not exaggerate to say that I left tears of joy, release, refreshment, and grace on every single page. It's that good. It's better—it's superb and so full of grace and truth that it has become a profound treasure. *Clay in the Potter's Hands* moved me to the depths of my soul.

—**ANDREW LAZO** speaker, priest, co-host of the "Pints with Jack Podcast," and co-editor of *Mere Christians: Inspiring Stories of Encounters with C. S. Lewis*

I find the general run of devotional books worse than useless; *Clay in the Potter's Hands* is a wonderful exception. A gifted writer who has thought long and hard about the Christian life and who has lived the biblical metaphor around which this work centers, she manages to be clear without being cloying, deep without being difficult, and spiritual without being sappy. She gives us everything the people who like devotional books are looking for without subjecting us to any of the things people who hate them are fleeing. This is a great achievement indeed.

—**DONALD T. WILLIAMS** pastor, missionary, and author of *Deeper Magic: The Theology Behind the Writings of C. S. Lewis*

This is a book to be savored. Devotional books like this one are rare; I don't remember the last time I read one that expresses the richness of Scripture with such simplicity, grace, and practical application. My own 'crack-pot' life experienced the shaping, restoring, and encouraging hand of the Potter through reading this book. I highly recommend the experience.

— **WILL VAUS** pastor of the First Congregational Church of Yarmouth and the author of *Mere Theology: A Guide to the Thought of C. S. Lewis*

I used Diana Glyer's *Clay in the Potter's Hands* for my ceramics classes. The students loved identifying with well-known biblical stories as they worked at mastering the potter's wheel.

— **SUSAN NEY** artist and professor, Azusa Pacific University

Most Christians have heard that God is the potter and we are the clay, but Diana Glyer, who has spent countless hours at the potter's wheel with her own hands saturated with clay, shows in this remarkable book that this saying is far more than a casual metaphor. As God hovers over his creation, centering us or shaping us or even restoring us from collapse, He may transform us in ways we never imagined. *Clay in the Potter's Hands* does a masterful job of revealing spiritual insights from an insider's perspective, as one potter considers the work of God the Master Artist.

— **JOSEPH BENTZ** author of *12 New Testament Passages That Changed the World*

As a Jesuit, I found this work very appealing. Each chapter is a movement from the wheel where clay is worked to a "wheel" where a healthy spiritual life is formed. The entire book could be read rather quickly, but I suggest that the reader savor each chapter as a daily prayer.

— **JOHN CHANDLER** priest at the Newman Center (Hawaii)

Clay in the Potter's Hands is a strong, extended metaphor that takes what is already a good analogy and makes it much more profound. When we hear the Apostle Paul say that we are like clay to God the Potter, we hardly realize that each stage of the process of shaping the artisan's work serves as a unique analog to something that God does in the process of shaping us. In our modern world of prefab housewares, that analogy could well have been lost, had not Glyer recaptured it for us.

—JAMES W. MILLER senior pastor of Real Life Church LA

Diana Glyer teaches like Jesus. This poetic parable of the pots got to my head and to my heart.

—GREG ANDERSON Graduate School Chaplain, Wheaton College

There is a tremendous need in each person's life to know God's reality, to feel his presence, to experience his guidance and love. Read *Clay in the Potter's Hands.* Like it did for me, it will open your eyes to the way God shapes us and loves us in a life-changing way. I cannot recommend a book on spiritual formation more highly to you—and your whole family!

—JOHN TRENT founder/president of The Center for Strong Families

Fascinating! As a potter, I could identify with the different stages of creating with clay, and as a Christian, I appreciated how this book ties each step into how God works in our lives. From the beginning to the end—God is able to use us—if we are yielded and still. Thank you for this insight and testimony of faith which has enriched my life.

—PAT BALLARD artist

CLAY
IN THE
POTTER'S
HANDS

CLAY IN THE POTTER'S HANDS

Revised and Expanded

DIANA PAVLAC GLYER

EDDY EFAW
STUDIO INSIGHTS

QUAY SAN
POTTERY & PHOTOGRAPHY

SQUARE HALO
BOOKS

©2025 Square Halo Books, Inc.
P.O. Box 18954 | Baltimore, MD 21206
www.SquareHaloBooks.com

Note: This is the first edition of Clay in the Potter's Hands
*to be published by Square Halo Books. Two earlier iterations
of this book (along with a workbook and leader's guide)
were originally produced by Tree House Studios.*

Except where otherwise noted, all Scripture references are from
The Holy Bible, New International Version (NIV), Copyright 2021 by
Biblica, Inc. Used by permission. All rights reserved worldwide.

ISBN 978-1-941106-38-9
Library of Congress Control Number: 2024944371

Printed in the United States of America

For Andrew Peterson, Pete Peterson,
and the rest of The Rabbit Room team.

*Our collaboration on this edition
began at Hutchmoot, and we continue
to be inspired by your wonderful work.
It's true: creativity thrives in community.*

CONTENTS

WHY CLAY?

I WILL PRAISE YOU,

FOR I AM FEARFULLY AND

WONDERFULLY MADE;

MARVELOUS ARE YOUR WORKS.

—PSALM 139:14 NKJV

I got into ceramics by accident—at least it seemed so at the time. As a
child, I was a big fan of a Disney movie called *The Three Lives of Thomasina*, in
which a cat named Thomasina becomes a bridge of understanding between a
father and his daughter. One of the characters in the film is Laurie, a weaver.
As I watched her pull and set the threads in line after line of color and
pattern, and as I listened to the sound of those large wooden shuttles rocking
back and forth, I discovered that weaving is a creative act that brings together

the very best of color and pattern and music and dance. I was enchanted by it. Years later, when I was a senior in high school, my counselor told me that I needed to sign up for an elective art class, and I jumped at the chance—I registered for Weaving 101.

When my schedule arrived, I noticed the mistake right away. Instead of Weaving 101, I was registered for Ceramics 101. Ceramics? I wasn't even sure what that *was*. Pouting and resentful, I decided to attend the class just once, then meet with my school counselor at the end of the day and explain that I couldn't possibly stay in that class. And then I'd rearrange things so that I'd get what I wanted in the first place.

But then I walked into that ceramics studio. I watched the potter spin a small lump of clay on the potter's wheel then pull it tall into a cylinder then shape it into a pot—in minutes, a magical transformation had taken place. The simple lump of clay was changed forever into something of worth and beauty. I was changed, too. I wanted to be a potter.

I never did get into that weaving class, but I have been working on the potter's wheel ever since. Being an artist is one of the deepest and highest things I do. Deepest because it so completely satisfies my heart. Highest because it lifts me, wordlessly, effortlessly, and happily, into communion with my Creator.

The Bible tells us that God is like a potter, and we are like clay. This beautiful image has special meaning for me, and I marvel at it every time I go to the ceramics studio, sit at the wheel, and begin my work. It seems to me that the more we know about clay, kilns, wheels, grog, firing, glazing, wedging, and the like, the more this spiritual picture becomes vivid and useful in our daily lives.

In this book, I share some of the rich meanings of this picture—God is the potter, we are the clay. And I will encourage you to reflect, to think and pray and discuss with others the significance of this transforming image in your own life. In addition, at the end of each chapter, my friend and fellow potter Eddy Efaw offers additional insights for those who want to *dig deeper* into the more technical aspects of how potters work on the potter's wheel.

What is it about clay in particular that makes the image of pottery making so persistent in Scripture and so appropriate as a metaphor for the way that God works in each of our lives?

GOD TELLS US THAT HE IS LIKE A POTTER WORKING WITH CLAY.

Throughout the Bible, God uses word pictures to tell us what he is like. God is like a loving shepherd. A good neighbor. A strong tower. Of all the pictures that God offers, one of the earliest and most persistent is this: God is like a potter, and we are like clay.

It starts in the beginning, with the creation story in the book of Genesis. God speaks, and all creation explodes into existence: Let there be light! Let there be land! Let there be water, plants, and living things! The scene is enormous, the work is glorious, the voice of the Lord is majestic, and the action is on the largest possible scale.

That is the glory of Genesis 1. But turn the page, and everything is changed. The theme that just a moment before was as big as the universe is suddenly small, quiet and very, very personal. You can almost hear a hush as God moves across the fresh, green world and begins a new work of creation:

> Then the Lord God formed a man from the dust of the ground
> and breathed into his nostrils the breath of life. (Genesis 2:7)

The Lord God formed the man. And look at how he did it. The word that is translated as "formed" comes from the Hebrew word *yatsar*, and *yatsar* refers to forming, stretching, squeezing, pressing, and molding something into a specific shape.

The word *yatsar* is quite literally the creative action of a potter working with clay—in fact, the very same word is used in Jeremiah 18 and 19, where the prophet goes to the house of the potter and watches as the clay is centered, opened, pulled, and shaped on the potter's wheel.

Throughout Scripture, there are many different images of God, an outpouring of images that help us understand what God is like. Here, in the Genesis account, in the beginning, God has chosen the image of the potter and the clay, and he repeats that image many times. Jeremiah 18:6 says we are like clay in the hands of a potter. In Isaiah 45:9, we are called clay, and in Romans 9:21, we are called lumps of clay. In Isaiah 29:16, 2 Corinthians 4:7, and 2 Timothy 2:20, we are called clay pots or jars of clay or earthen vessels. In Isaiah 64:8, the prophet speaks to God, saying,

> We are the clay, you are the potter; we are all the work of your hand. (Isaiah 64:8)

We are all the work of God's hand. What attributes of potters and clay in particular help us understand why God would describe his work in this way?

THE POTTER STOOPS LOW
OVER THE POT TO SHAPE IT.

In order to work at the potter's wheel, the potter must stoop low, sit down, and settle in.

The potter's wheel is surrounded, almost embraced, by the potter's body. In Genesis 1:2, we read that the Holy Spirit hovers over the face of the waters. In creation, God steps down. Comes near. Bends low. Hovers close.

This is true of creation; it is also true of incarnation. Jesus came down from heaven, took on flesh, and dwelt among us. Jesus reached out and touched lepers, hugged sinners, held children. The same God who flung stars across the skies wrapped a towel around his waist, knelt down, and washed the feet of his disciples.

The potter must stoop low over the pot to shape it; pottery making depicts a creator who came down from heaven and daily draws near.

CLAY GETS ALL OVER THE POTTER
AS THE POTTER WORKS WITH CLAY.

Some art forms allow for the artist to work at a polite distance. A sculptor might stand with hammer and chisel, chipping away at a block of marble. A painter holds brushes to apply paint to canvas. But when I work with clay, it soaks into my hands, slips under my fingernails, splatters my clothes, gets caught in my hair. I was sitting at a formal luncheon recently and turned to introduce myself to a student sitting at our table. She grinned as she said, "I hardly recognize you now, but we have met before. I visited your art class a few months ago. The last time I saw you, Professor, you were covered with clay!"

It's true: as I reach out to touch the clay, it gets all over me. And throughout my day, it seems that I am always finding smudges of clay here and there. No matter how long I spend cleaning up at the sink, inevitably I discover (too late!) that I have somehow missed a spot, and the clay still marks my hands. I can't escape it.

When I've been sitting and working at the wheel for a while, the water saturates my hands, and the wet, slippery clay works itself into the folds of skin at my knuckles. It tucks itself into the spaces between my fingers. I can't get away from it.

Even more—eventually, as my hands have been immersed in art-making for a while, tiny, tiny bits of clay work themselves into the very pores of my skin. And stay there. I can't avoid it. In Isaiah 49:15–16, the Lord says,

> I will not forget you! See, I have engraved you on the palms of my hands.

In a similar way, the clay becomes quite literally etched into the potter's skin.

Clay gets all over the potter as the potter works with the clay; pottery making illustrates the Maker's intimacy with his creation.

CLAY POTS RETAIN EVIDENCE OF THE ONE WHO MADE THEM.

Acts 14:15 is clear: God has made "the heavens and the earth and the sea and everything in them." The passage goes on to declare that God has not left us without clear and abiding evidence of himself, his goodness, and his creative hand in our lives.

The earth is the Lord's, and it reflects his nature.

Each work of art bears the mark and reveals the nature of the one who made it. But clay is a very responsive medium. Ben Carter, a master potter, emphasizes this quality, saying "Clay has a knack for recording the feelings of the maker."

But there's more. It's not just that these clay vessels reflect the personality of the potter. There's more. You can go to a museum and see clay vessels that are thousands of years old. Look closely: despite the passage of time, there are actual marks pressed into the clay. Think of it—although those human fingers turned to dust ages ago, the clear imprint of those finger marks remains. Compared to other art forms, clay shows forth those literal fingerprints more clearly. Every one of us bears *imago Dei*, the image of our Creator, in the same way that the work of art shaped from clay bears the mark of the one who made it.

Clay responds sensitively and permanently to the touch of the potter; pottery-making represents God's certain touch on our lives.

REFLECTION & DISCUSSION

God is a creator, an artist, a maker. Think back on a time you have made things—anything, from rebuilding a carburetor to writing a song to coloring with crayons. What steps did you take to complete the work? Did you see your personality reflected in the work? Did you sense that your creativity was a divine gift, a reflection of the creative nature of God? In what ways?

Make a list of several times that you have clearly seen the fingerprints of God in the circumstances of your life. Then take time to thank God for it!

.   .   .

PRAYER

You who are the King of all creation have stooped low
to care for me. You who oversee all galaxies have become
intimately involved in everything that concerns me.
You are eager to enter into the mess of my life as you
patiently shape and form me into your likeness.
You who are the mighty one still bear the marks
of your creation on your hands. Open my eyes, God,
to see you more clearly in this season of my life
than I ever have before. I wait expectantly for fresh
insight into who you are and who I am in you. Amen.

STUDIO INSIGHTS

Pottery making is an ancient art. It is also a worldwide pursuit. Through the ages and around the world, potters have used clay to make vessels that are beautiful and useful. One of the earliest utilitarian pieces was found in a cave in southeastern China and dated to 18,000 BCE. Petrified rice was found near it, hinting at its intended use.

The use of clay-based ceramics spread from Asia to the Middle East and then from there to Europe. Clay is one of the most abundant of all raw materials, and it can be found throughout the world. It quickly became a popular material for creating storage jars, cooking pots, tiles, bricks, and artwork. These items were generally fired at low temperatures in shallow fire pits dug into the ground.

The first wheel-thrown pottery was developed in Egypt around 3,500 BCE. Using a wheel made it easy to produce sturdy vessels very quickly. Decorative figures were added by stamping designs into the soft clay or painting images onto the surface. In ancient Greece, potters perfected the use of red and black minerals to decorate the clay surface with detailed images, often using this technique to illustrate stories of battles, heroes, and gods.

Today, Jingdezhen in China, Khurja in India, and Stoke-on-Trent in England are renowned as centers for ceramics. But pottery making is popular around the world. When you complete the construction of a coil pot or glaze a wheel-thrown bowl, you are connecting to an ancient craft and participating in one of the oldest and most pervasive forms of art.

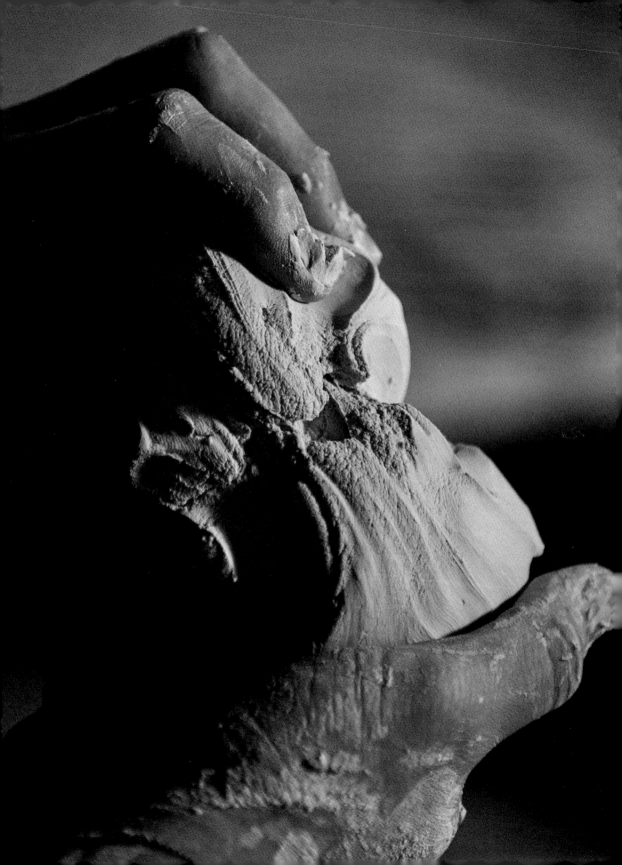

I I

SEARCHING

THE POTTER ACTIVELY SEEKS

THE CLAY AND REJOICES

WHEN IT IS FOUND.

It is still early in the morning as the potter finishes the last bits of breakfast. He clears the dishes, picks up an old walking stick, and heads out through the woods behind his home. He walks along the creek bank and then climbs the narrow path that leads him through the surrounding hills. He is looking for clay.

Clay is formed in the earth when rain falls on rocks, dissolving minerals, oxides, and organic materials. They combine and form deposits along the riverbank or settle at the bottom of a shallow lake or stream. Silt and dirt accumulate on top of it, plants take root, and there it remains. Hidden.

Hidden until the potter goes looking for it, searching through forgotten pathways, digging through layers of debris.

When a potter searches for clay, he is like a miner who tunnels through the earth to find a deposit of gold or copper, silver or jewels (Prov. 2:4). He is like a merchant who looks for fine pearls (Matt. 13:45–46). A fisherman who searches the sea for a catch of fish (Matt. 13:47–49). A woman who carefully seeks a lost coin (Luke 15:8–10). A father who looks longingly day after day for his son who is lost (Luke 15:11–31). Or a shepherd who goes after that one little lamb:

> Suppose one of you has a hundred sheep and loses one of them. Doesn't he leave the ninety-nine in the open country and go after the lost sheep until he finds it? And when he finds it, he joyfully puts it on his shoulders and goes home. Then he calls his friends and neighbors together and says, "Rejoice with me; I have found my lost sheep." (Luke 15:4–6)

In Ezekiel 34:15–16, God shows us more of this shepherd's heart: "I myself will tend my sheep," says the Lord. "I will search for the lost and bring back the strays. I will bind up the injured and strengthen the weak." God loves us, values us, eagerly seeks for us, and rejoices over us when we are found.

The Good Shepherd knows his sheep—each is unique in many ways. Clay is like that, too. Depending on the particular mix of minerals and other raw materials, each kind of clay takes on a unique quality and character. The texture will vary from coarse and gritty to silky and smooth. It may be porous or dense, sticky or crumbly, soft or solid. Even the color differs from clay to clay, ranging from bright white to pale ivory to rich red terra cotta, chocolate brown, and midnight black.

The specific qualities of the clay—its porosity, plasticity, appearance, firing temperature—all these things will vary according to the qualities inherent in that particular clay. These qualities are built into the very composition of the clay's nature.

The type of clay with its inherent nature is called the clay body.

A good potter recognizes the unique and beautiful qualities of each type of clay. The amount of pressure that the clay can tolerate and the amount of heat that it needs to reach its potential—these factors and more will vary from clay to clay, and the good potter understands the differences.

Chances are you know a family whose kids are very different from one another. One child is placid, another fussy. One wakes at a whisper, the other sleeps through a thunderstorm. One is sunny and cheerful; another thoughtful, moody. One is impatient, restless, ready for any new thing. Another is cautious, resistant to change.

My family is like that. When I was a child, I was a typical firstborn in many ways: Sensitive. Obedient. I was like porcelain. When I did something wrong, all my mom had to do was give me "that look" and say my full name. I knew I was in trouble. I would dissolve into tears, devastated.

My sister, on the other hand, is made of sterner stuff. She is, in many ways, a typical second born: Resilient. Collected. She is more like earthenware. When she did something wrong, Mom could pull out all the stops—scolding, swatting, threatening, punishing. My sister knew she was in trouble. But she would just look Mom in the eye and shrug, unfazed.

Wise parents know how to adapt to the particular temperament of each child; in order to be fair, they must handle each individual a little differently. Wise teachers know how to adjust the requirements of a class to the interests and abilities of their students. Wise potters know how to adapt pressure, speed, water, and heat to the particular temperament of the clay.

God in all his wisdom knows what is best. He has searched me and known me and called me by name.

REFLECTION & DISCUSSION

God has been seeking you all of your life. If you have responded to his call and been found by him, take time now to thank him for the way he has made you his own. If you have never responded, take time now to consider what it might mean for you, a wandering lamb, to be found and taken home to his fold. Then find someone who can tell you more about the Good Shepherd who loves you.

Each type of clay has unique qualities; each of us is unique in personality, abilities, and gifts. Spend some time journaling about the ways in which you are unique, like clay.

Then ask God to show you how these qualities are strengths that he can use.

.   .   .

PRAYER

God, in your goodness, keep seeking after me and drawing me to your side. Thank you that you see in me something of infinite worth. I want to be used by you to do something of great importance. Show me how to become available to you so that your miraculous hand can do mighty things on Earth through me. Amen.

STUDIO INSIGHTS

Common clay can be found below the first few feet of topsoil. It can be instructive to seek out clay deposits in your local area. How do you locate raw clay? Look for a dried creek bed containing cracked clay across its surface; look along the bottom of cliffs or rock outcroppings where water runoff carries clay particles; check construction sites where workers have dug through layers of topsoil and revealed rich veins of clay. You'll recognize it by the way the color contrasts with the surrounding soil. And you'll notice that the texture is sticky and smooth instead of sandy or crumbly.

There are three main types of clay. **Earthenware** or terracotta is the most common. It contains a lot of iron oxide, giving it a rusty red or orange color. Earthenware tends to be rough-textured and porous, so potters use it for thicker, chunkier pieces. Gardeners appreciate earthenware because it provides good drainage for plants and flowers.

Stoneware is a smooth and durable high-fire clay. It is stronger and more chip-resistant than earthenware, and that's why it is a common choice for dinnerware and coffee mugs.

Porcelain is a light, white clay with a soft, fine texture. It absorbs water quickly and can be challenging for beginners to work with. A skilled potter can create porcelain vessels that are so thin that you can see light shining through.

When you are working with different clays, remember that the inherent qualities of each one make a significant contribution to the beauty and functionality of the unique pieces you are creating.

| | |

PREPARING

THE POTTER PULLS THE
CLAY OUT OF THE EARTH
AND PREPARES IT.

By the time the potter finds the clay and digs it out of the ground, it has been pressed into the earth for quite a while. As a result, certain impurities have become embedded in it. There are small rocks, twigs, bits of leaf and bone, all the result of having been pressed against the world. Many of these things are very small and don't seem to be particularly significant. The clay looks great: clean and smooth and pure. But if these foreign objects are not removed, there will be serious consequences in the life of the pot.

A little sliver of wood, a tiny stone, a pocket of air, or seed, sand, root, or twig—it is possible that such things will stay hidden for a long, long time. But in the firing process, in the heat of the kiln, nothing can stay hidden for long.

Impurities will react in the heat. The pot will explode, sometimes cracking or splitting, sometimes collapsing into a heap of rubble, and sometimes flying apart with so much force that sharp bits of clay are embedded into the sides of the pottery around it.

You see, pots are shaped individually, one by one on the potter's wheel, but they generally go through the firing process together. Hidden debris becomes evident in the testing by fire, and the result can be an entire batch of pots all scarred and ruined by one small, personal, private flaw.

I know of families that relate to one another very well most of the time. But then, suddenly, tough times come. A job is lost. A child becomes ill. Finances become tight. And some small issue—a sin that was hidden, a situation that was ignored, a personal habit that was carefully managed in the good times— becomes a kind of time bomb.

And individuals and families are blown apart.

The truth is that even good times can become the testing ground for character flaws and unfinished business. How many times has something as exciting as a family vacation become the opportunity for God to turn up the heat and see what is really in our hearts?

Flaws and impurities will come to light in the fire of testing, but, in general, most of them are discovered and dealt with earlier, as the clay is cleaned and prepared.

This is for the good of the pot, and it is good for the safety of the other pots around it. But it also serves to protect the potter. Stones, sticks, and other small items become dangerous in the shaping process. This debris has to be dealt with. Can you picture it? Overlook something small and sharp, and it will scratch or even puncture the potter's hands.

Because this is such a serious matter, the wise potter takes extra care at this stage of the process. The clay is carefully examined, and stones, sticks, and other materials are carefully removed. It might even be put through a screen in order to eliminate even the smallest thing that might be harmful.

The clay is carefully cleaned and then it is wedged, a process that looks a lot like kneading dough. It is an important step, requiring patient attention from the potter. It involves a satisfying rhythm of pressing, turning, pressing, turning.

I like to think of it as clay brought into harmony. Debris is removed. Air bubbles are released. And these quiet, rhythmic, repeated motions create a consistent texture throughout all parts of the clay. Any parts that are stiff or mushy are evened out as moisture is distributed evenly throughout the clay. Isn't it interesting that water, moisture, is used throughout the Bible as a symbol of the Holy Spirit!

I had a recent experience that helped to remind me of what it means for even the smallest things in our lives to be carefully dealt with. I was on campus at the university where I teach, and one of my students came to my office and asked if she could talk with me. Her eyes filled with tears as we sat down, and she blurted out, "I'm so ashamed of what I've done! I haven't been able to sleep or anything. I saw you today and my heart started beating so fast it scared me."

I didn't have any idea what she meant—I couldn't imagine what could be causing such distress. She lowered her eyes and said "I cheated on my last quiz. I added an extra answer right after we graded them in class, right before we turned them in. It was only two extra points. It was such a small thing. But I don't care anymore about what happens to my grades. I just need to let you know that I was wrong, and I'm so sorry."

Cheating on a daily quiz? Such a small thing. But coming to me to confess it? That's huge.

I thanked her for her courage and told her I would deduct those points and adjust her grade. Then I thanked her again and told her that her desire to maintain absolute integrity filled me with admiration. "You are a model of what it is like to walk in Christ, sensitive to his word, quick to obey the prompting of his Spirit. That gift of a sensitive soul is one of the most important gifts God has given you. Don't ever let anything compromise that strong desire to make things right."

I know something about the damage that even small things can cause.

REFLECTION & DISCUSSION

Are there things in your life, large or small, that God wants to remove from your life because they hurt his heart and harm others?

Are there people you need to talk to in order to settle a matter that has caused stress, tension, shame, or uneasiness? Is there someone you need to reach out to in order to make things right?

. . .

PRAYER

O God, there are things in my life that I thought were private issues or insignificant matters. But now I see that they can be dangerous. They hurt me, hurt you, hurt others. I have not dealt with them the way I should. I confess that I've been wrong. Trusting in your goodness, I give you full permission to remove _____ from my life. I surrender it to you, knowing that even small things will pierce your hands. I surrender it to you, convinced that even small things can hurt my sisters and my brothers. Remove the rocks, sticks, and sharp stones that have been worked into my soul, and fill the empty places with healing balm and the presence of your Holy Spirit, in Jesus' name. Let this be my prayer day by day. Amen.

STUDIO INSIGHTS

These days, most potters don't dig their clay out of the ground: they order it from a supplier, and it arrives clean and prepared in large bags. Commercial clay still needs to be wedged in order to disperse hard and soft clay particles and ensure a consistent texture.

There are two styles of wedging: spiral and ram's head. Experiment with both, and over time, you will discover the style you like best. You will also find that one style may work better than the other depending on the amount of clay or the particular clay body. No matter the technique, the goal is the same: a ball of clay with a perfectly even texture, no air bubbles, and no impurities.

Week after week, as you work on the wheel--centering, opening, shaping, trimming, joining, or carving—clay scraps will surely accumulate. Your studio will have a reclaim bucket to gather these scraps along with uneven cylinders or work that did not make the grade: pots that wobble, warp, collapse, or fail to suit. Add them all to the reclaim bucket. These clay scraps will be dissolved in water. In small studios, this reclaimed clay will be partially dried on a plaster slab and then wedged. Larger studios run it through a pugmill that mixes and then extrudes usable clay.

Be careful, though. As artists work together in a classroom or studio, foreign objects can be inadvertently dropped in the reclaim bucket. A piece of an old sponge, a twist tie, or the shard of a fired pot can find its way into the remixed clay. These can ruin the project, injure the potter, or damage the equipment.

From the very beginning, as you are working to master the art of pottery making, take care as you wedge, shape, and recycle your clay.

COMMITTING

THE CLAY IS FIRMLY ATTACHED TO THE POTTER'S WHEEL.

Once a ball of clay has been cleaned and wedged, the potter pats it into an oval shape. Then, with a motion that is swift and deliberate, the potter holds the clay above the center of the flat, round surface of the potter's wheel head and brings it down with a loud smack.

Why such a sudden, strong, almost violent action? Because the clay has to be completely attached to the potter's wheel in order for the potter to work with it. Fully fastened. Completely committed.

Moments of commitment are all around us: They are clear, measurable, memorable, and often powerful. A marriage ceremony. A job contract. A license to practice medicine or law or pastoral ministry. The vows that lead to the monastic life. Throughout our lives, all of us are brought to precise and specific moments of decision, moments that are often accompanied by a ceremony or a ritual.

Each one represents a swift and deliberate point of commitment. I remember when my godsons were dedicated to God and, in a beautiful ceremony, I made a vow to pray for them, care for them, and invest time and resources into their lives. The pastor used this baptismal liturgy to explain my role:

> It is your privilege and responsibility then, after they have been baptized, to remember your godchild in your prayers, remind them of their baptism, and whenever possible, support them in mind and heart, especially if they should lose their parents, so they may be brought up in the true knowledge and fear of God. Do you intend gladly and willingly to assume this responsibility? If so answer, "Yes, with the help of God."

Making that commitment was easy. After all, those baby boys were so tiny, so sweet, and so uncomplicated.

But now I am faced with a commitment to keep. My precious godsons have grown. They are scattered across the country; they have families of their own. Keeping in touch with them, keeping up with them, remembering them in my prayers, and supporting them "in mind and heart" is complicated. Commitment was swift and easy.

But faithful persistence is long and it's hard.

Just as there are things that can compromise the strength of our personal commitments, so there are things that compromise the tight commitment that keeps the clay firmly attached to the wheel. When the potter begins to work on the wheel, too much water may slip under the clay. Or, in the process of attaching the clay, a pocket of air might get trapped underneath. These can damage the seal that holds the clay tightly to the spinning potter's wheel. If this happens, then as soon as the potter starts to apply a little pressure, the clay will slide sideways and fly off. In order for the potter to work, nothing can be spinning out of control, slopping over the sides, slipping to the floor, running for the door.

The only way for the potter to work on the clay is for the clay to be firmly attached to the wheel. And then for it to stay there. In the same way, following God means cultivating faithfulness. He tells us we shouldn't put our hands to the plow and then look back—the work gets done with commitment and then focused, faithful, persistent devotion (Luke 9:62).

I think of a doctoral student working to prepare for comprehensive exams—day after day, week after week. And sometimes she wonders if it's worth it.

I think of a scientist, patiently going to the lab day after day, working on research, taking intricate, repeated, painstaking steps.

A mother working with a child who's unruly.

An athlete training for a contest that is months, even years, away.

A physical therapist working with a patient, struggling together to restore movement to an injured hand.

God has taken the initiative: like a potter who seeks after the clay, God has sought us, drawn us to himself, cleaned us up, and prepared us. Throughout our lives, we find that we are now being given the opportunity to respond. We commit our lives wholeheartedly to Christ. And having made that commitment, we persevere. We resist the temptation to give up. We stick with it, even when it becomes inconvenient, annoying, uncomfortable, or dangerous to do so.

REFLECTION & DISCUSSION

Has God convinced you of any area of your life that is not going well because you haven't made a decisive commitment, fully surrendering that aspect of life to God? If so, take time to make that commitment sure.

Think about the long-term projects that you are in the midst of. List them. Then ask God to strengthen your resolve and help you finish well.

PRAYER

Forgive me, Gracious Heavenly Father,
for the times I have broken my commitments
because the situation just got too hard.
Show me if I need to take steps to repair
any damage I have caused. And now, rekindle
hope in my heart to face the challenges that are
before me this day. Give me the strength and
courage to persevere in those things that you have
called me to do. Then let me run the race, this day,
with cheerful endurance. And when I come to the
end of my life, let me say with the Apostle Paul,
"I have fought the good fight, I have finished the race,
I have kept the faith" (2 Tim. 4:7). Amen.

STUDIO INSIGHTS

When you attach clay to the wheel head, you are creating a strong seal so that the clay stays in place. Be careful to avoid problems that interfere with that seal, such as a puddle of water or an air pocket. If you begin with the clay reasonably centered, placing it near the center of the wheel head and patting it into place, it will take less effort to finesse the centering process.

Once the clay is attached, take a moment to check that the bottom edge is not flared out; tap or press lightly around the bottom edges. Good! You are ready to set the wheel on a medium-fast speed and begin centering.

While some potters attach the clay directly onto the wheel head, others prefer to use a bat. This is a plastic, masonite, wooden, or plaster disc that is affixed to the wheel head before the clay is thrown onto it.

Some pottery wheels have built-in bat pins: these raised bolts are designed to be used with specially designed bats: these have holes that fit exactly onto the bolts and hold the bat tightly to the wheel. A thin scrap of fabric—an old scrap of T-shirt or a chamois—may be placed underneath the bat to stabilize it.

Double commitment: the bat is attached to the wheel, and the clay is attached to the bat. The advantage of using a bat? Once the piece is finished, you can simply pick up the bat with the pot on it and set the whole thing aside to dry. This is especially helpful when making plates or bowls that have wide bases. Bats made of wood or plaster have the added advantage of pulling moisture from the bottom of the pot while it is drying. This equalizes the drying process and helps keep your piece from cracking.

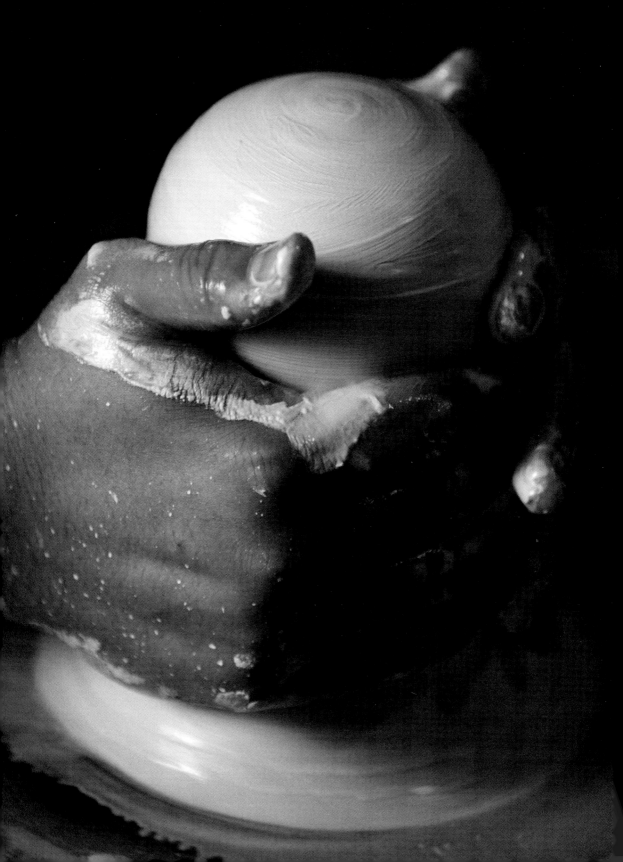

CENTERING

THE POTTER SPINS THE
POTTER'S WHEEL AND
CENTERS THE CLAY.

When I am working with students, they are always looking for shortcuts. But mastering a creative art takes time, and the beginning steps may be tedious and frustrating: the painter stretches canvas, the pianist practices scales, the dancer repeats a step or a turn, an actor memorizes lines. The one part of the process that causes my art students the most frustration is the time it takes to center the clay. It's not that hard. It just takes a really long time.

Once the clay is attached to the wheel, the potter spins it. Most potters use electric wheels. The speed of the wheel is controlled by a pedal that looks just like the gas pedal in your car. As the pedal is pressed, the wheel spins faster or slower, depending on the kind of work the potter is doing. Some potters prefer kick wheels or treadle wheels; these are powered and controlled by the movements of the potter's feet.

The process of making a pot on the potter's wheel is called throwing. It is a funny term, but it has a long history in our language. The idea of throwing, or a throw, means shaping something as it turns. It is the turning or spinning of the wheel, the centrifugal force, that the potter uses to shape a lump of clay into a cup, vase, or bowl.

But first, the clay must be centered; that is to say, every part and every aspect of it must be lined up with the very heart of the wheel.

When the lump of clay first starts to spin, it is obviously off-center—it is oddly shaped, it wobbles back and forth, it follows its own path. The potter takes a little water to moisten his or her hands, then presses them against the spinning clay, pushing the clay closer to the wheel head, smoothing uneven places, pressing bumpy edges.

The clay wobbles, but the potter's hands are held steady, guiding the clay into the center one revolution at a time. The potter uses just enough pressure to center all parts of the clay. If the clay is stiff or the lump is large, it may take quite a bit of pressure to make the clay obey.

It also may take a surprisingly long time. And when you are watching a potter work on this step, it may look like nothing much is happening. It is easy to express impatience at this point in the process: "Aren't we done yet? Didn't you just do that a minute ago? Are you sure we're getting anywhere?"

Centering takes time. But it is absolutely critical that every aspect of the clay is lined up. One small wobble now will spell disaster later—it won't affect the shape of things for the moment, but it will bump the whole pot out of kilter if it is not lined up right now. All of the clay must be centered. Like a symphony with no unnecessary notes. Like a gymnast perfectly controlled down to the tips of her fingers and her toes.

This idea of being centered is a powerful one for me, for my life is very busy, and I confess that unless I am very, very careful, I go running off in all directions. I have yet to master what it means to live in the absolute center, in the Great Shalom, in the peace of God. The Hebrew word shalom is a powerful word meaning absolute tranquility. It means doing things with natural ease, not with frantic force or fearful striving. It means responding to life's challenges with a sense of optimism and resilience. It is a sense in my body and my soul of well-being, safety, harmony, and vibrant health. To be at ease, inside and out. Shalom. Aligned.

While shalom includes all of this, the root of the word is wholeness. When Jesus instructs us to be perfect, he means we are to be whole, mature, grown-up, living in the fullness of all that God intends for us. Shalom. Complete.

When I think about the rich meaning of the word shalom, I am tempted to get overwhelmed all over again. All of this seems more than I can bear, and it threatens to set me to even more fretting and striving. Isn't it ironic: remind me of the gift of shalom, and I am tempted to write "get some shalom" on my to-do list right after "do the laundry" and "buy eggs and milk."

It helps when I remember the powerful promise of Philippians 1:6:

He who began a good work in you will carry it on to completion.

God began it. God will complete it. It's not supposed to be on my to-do list. It's already on his. Shalom is the peaceful fruit of God's initiative, God's labor, God's faithfulness, and not my own. That wobbly, bumpy, misshapen lump of clay rests under the skill of the potter's hands, and as a result, it becomes smooth, solid, and wholly centered. And so it is with my soul.

REFLECTION & DISCUSSION

Reflect on your schedule this past week. Was it calm and centered, characterized by joy and peace, ease and strength? Or was it marred by fearful striving? Were you able to find moments of *shalom* despite the push and pull of life's circumstances?

Now get specific: What changes do you need to make in your life so that the Great Shalom, the peace of God, is an ever-increasing part of your daily life?

.   .   .

PRAYER

Lord God, I don't want to be tossed to and fro
by my circumstances. I want to rest under your hand,
quiet, content, strong, and centered. Rather than
trying harder to fix all this, I choose to slow down,
breathe deeply, and trust the work of your hands.
Amen.

STUDIO INSIGHTS

When you watch an experienced potter centering the clay, it looks effortless. However, the process takes a while to master. Your body posture makes a big difference. Be sure that your stool is as close to the wheel as possible and that you are leaning over the clay rather than sitting up straight. Press your legs right up against the splash pan; anchor your feet to the ground; steady your forearms on your legs. This closeness to the clay will allow you to optimize the weight of your body to help you shape the clay.

Then set the wheel at a medium-fast speed. It is tempting to think of centering as just pushing the clay into the middle. In fact, you will be working with the centrifugal force of the spinning wheel to raise the ball of clay up into a cone shape and then back down.

First, **cone up**: Add a little water to the clay and to your hands. Then wrap both hands around the ball of clay, squeezing inward. The clay will move upward, changing into a cone shape, and it will naturally begin to find its center.

Next, **cone down**: with one hand on the top of the clay and the other steadying the side, keep the clay aligned and centered as you press it back down into a rounded lump. Slow and steady, but firm and strong.

Continue these steps, coning up and then down again, until the clay is centered. Not sure if you are there yet? Hold a finger by the side of the lump as it spins and look closely to see if the sides are perfectly aligned. Or try resting both hands gently on the clay and close your eyes as it spins. Centered clay feels like it's barely moving. When you are learning to center, take your time. It's not a fancy step, nor an obvious one, but it is important. Practice and be patient. Centering takes time.

OPENING

THE POTTER PRESSES INTO THE CENTER AND OPENS THE CLAY.

From the potter's point of view, this next step is just about the most beautiful step in the whole process. The clay has been cleaned and prepared and firmly attached to the wheel. It is perfectly centered. It looks good, and it feels good. Smooth. Round. Beautiful.

There is only one problem with this lovely lump of clay. I heard Jon Mourglia say it well in a pottery demonstration he did years ago. He said, "This lump of clay is full of itself!" And he's right. The lump is solid through and through. There is no opening that will turn that lump into a bowl, a cup, or a vase. There is no opening into which I may put my Cheerios, pour my coffee, arrange my daffodils. The lump is lovely and it is centered, but at this point in the process, there is too much in the way. It is of no use to me at all.

In order to transform that clay into something I can use, I have to open a hole in the middle of it. I rest my left hand lightly on the outside of the clay; I use the fingers of my right hand to press into the top of the clay. Pressing down and pulling out, I move the clay aside and open up an empty place.

Empty places. How carefully we arrange our lives to make sure we avoid empty places! Unscheduled Friday nights. Long Sunday afternoons. Silent car rides. Quiet living rooms. Still office spaces.

We can hardly stand it. We turn up the music, check social media, plow through the latest episodes of our favorite shows. We overstuff our closets, our desktops, our calendars. Because, to tell the truth, we hate empty places. We fill them up as fast as we can with whatever we can get our hands on.

Sometimes we stuff them with sin—we numb the anxious feelings with alcohol, pills, drugs, or sensual indulgence.

Or sometimes we just overdo it in order to soothe ourselves—recreational shopping, extra desserts, junky magazines, hour after hour of video games or sports radio or scrolling through social media.

Or rather than sin or overdo, sometimes we just keep our lives noisy and crowded, filled to overflowing with good things: service projects, ministry opportunities, wholesome books, visits with friends.

The problem is that we are not very useful when we are full of ourselves. God can fill us and use us only when we clear the way, leave some room, and cultivate an open, empty space. How do we create empty space? Since emptiness and quiet can be frightening, we might start small. Turn off the car radio on the way to work and use that time to reflect and pray. Resist the temptation to stream Netflix as "background noise" and put on some instrumental music instead. Go for a walk (no phones, no music) and quietly observe the beauty all around you.

Pray, worship, watch, listen. God can speak to us in many ways. In Job 38–40, we read that God answered Job out of the whirlwind. And so he can. But more often, it seems that we must make room in our schedules, our homes, and our hearts so that we can hear his voice (Ps. 116:1), recognize his voice (Judg. 18), listen carefully to his voice (Exod. 15:26), pay attention to his voice (Exod. 23:21), and obey his voice (Exod. 19:5).

More often, we are not so much like Job as like the prophet Elijah, recorded in 1
Kings 19:11. God tells Elijah,

> Go out and stand on the mountain in the presence of the LORD, for the LORD is about to pass by.

Because he knows the Lord and loves the Lord, Elijah quickly responds. He goes, and there he stands.

> Then a great and powerful wind tore the mountains apart and shattered the rocks before the LORD, but the LORD was not in the wind. After the wind there was an earthquake, but the LORD was not in the earthquake. After the earthquake came a fire, but the LORD was not in the fire. And after the fire came a gentle whisper. When Elijah heard it, he pulled his cloak over his face and went out and stood at the mouth of the cave. (1 Kings 19:12–13)

And there he met with God.

Our daily lives are often tossed by wind, touched by fire, shaken from the ground. It is not easy to struggle through it all, pressing in to the quiet place where we can hear the still, small voice of God. There are disciplines that help us to grow in this way; in fact, most of the ancient disciplines of the church are designed to make space for God to pour in more of himself. There are four disciplines that I have found particularly helpful.

SOLITUDE

Solitude is making specific time to be alone, away from other people and the voices of co-workers, family members, television shows, podcasts, books, and articles. It is deliberately taking a retreat all by myself, perhaps a morning in the park, a day trip to the mountains, or a weekend at an abbey or cabin or hotel. It may be the very simple discipline of a morning walk three days a week, or an evening habit of sitting on the back porch with closed eyes and open heart.

SILENCE

When I seek solitude, I take a break from other voices. But when I seek silence, I take a break from my own voice. I look for occasions when I can silence emails, texts, and phone calls in order to go through some part of a day deliberately without talking. Another aspect of it is to become aware of the chatter in my head—the excuse-making, the schedule planning, the hypothetical conversations with other people, the scolding and complaining I direct toward myself. When I exercise the discipline of silence, I deliberately hush.

FASTING

To fast is to give up food for a time. It reminds me how dependent and needy I am. I have struggled with fasting as a discipline because I really don't understand why it is so powerful, and why it is so often seen as a necessary adjunct to effective prayer. For me, much of the power in fasting is simply this: it forces me to pay attention to feelings of emptiness. And when I acknowledge those feelings and allow myself to fully experience them, I am better able to give them completely to God. Otherwise, I tend to stuff them down, ignore them, cover them up, or find some way to medicate myself against them. And when I muster the courage to admit my pain and fear of emptiness, it provides an opening for God to meet me and heal me.

RELEASING

One of the areas of my life that I constantly struggle with is materialism. I like recreational shopping, what some folks call "retail therapy." It is so easy for my focus to shift from heavenly matters to earthly ones. As an antidote, I regularly go through my belongings and give things away. In the forty days of Lent, as part of my preparation for Easter, I give away forty things as a discipline. In preparation for Christmas, I take a day to "prepare him room," and I go through the house, gathering up things that I don't really need anymore. Then I box them up to donate them to charity.

These four disciplines—solitude, silence, fasting, and releasing—are powerful tools. There are others, and you might take a look at the recommended reading list at the end of this book for suggestions on what to read to learn more about them. Ultimately, each discipline serves the same purpose: creating an empty space into which God can pour those good things he has prepared for us from before the foundation of the world.

REFLECTION & DISCUSSION

To what extent have you filled up your schedule as a way of avoiding the scary feeling of being empty? Can you identify any specific things that you need to push out of the way to make room for the whisper of God?

Search your heart and then your calendar: Can you set aside a specific time for solitude, silence, fasting, and/or releasing sometime in the next month?

PRAYER

God, it is true—I am better at hanging on to things
than letting them go. As a result, my life has gotten
so crowded that there is little room for the new things
that you want to pour into my life. To be honest,
there really isn't very much room for you, either.
I don't like to admit it, but I am an awful lot
like that innkeeper in Bethlehem whose place
was full to overflowing, and when the King of Glory
came to call, there was no room. Forgive my
self-indulgence, heal my fears, and teach me
to be available and open to you. Amen.

STUDIO INSIGHTS

There are two basic strategies that potters use to open the centered lump of clay. Many beginners find it easiest to rest their hands to the right and left of the clay and press into the center with their thumbs, opening a hole. Others prefer to hold one hand on the outside of the clay and use the fingers of the other hand to press in and open out. This is a chance to experiment and see what works best for you.

Whichever way you choose, be sure to have an ample amount of water on both the clay and on your hands. Any dryness at this stage will snag and then bump the clay off-center. A sponge can be very useful to help keep the surface moist and collect excess slurry that may accumulate.

The sponge may also be used to absorb any excess water that puddles in the bottom of your vessel. Wet clay is quite absorbent. Water left in the bottom will cause splits and cracks. Too much water on the sides can weaken the walls and make the clay too soft to hold its shape.

Your goal when opening? Almost every form starts with a straight cylinder and is shaped from there, whether you are creating a vase, cup, mug, or teapot. Start with a straight cylinder: the outside of the clay and the inside of the clay should form vertical lines: smooth, straight, and parallel.

Remember, opening doesn't happen in one swift motion. When you are opening the clay, take your time. If you rush the process now, all the hard work of centering could be lost.

GROUNDING

THE POTTER CREATES
A FLAT, STABLE FOUNDATION.

Once the lump of clay has been centered and opened, the potter needs to widen and strengthen the bottom of the vessel. This involves three actions in quick succession:

OPEN OUT THE FLOOR

When potters reach the right depth, they curl their fingers and pull outward from the center of the wheel to create a flat base across the inside of the pot. This establishes the interior width of the final form: a narrow vase, a tall pitcher, a wide bowl.

COMPRESS THE FLOOR

Once the floor is established, the potter compresses the base by running a finger or wooden tool across the bottom and firmly pressing down. Compressing the floor of the pot establishes a strong, straight line and helps to avoid cracks that can develop later.

SPONGE-DRY THE FLOOR

Even a small amount of standing water can seep into the floor of the pot and weaken it. The potter uses a sponge inside the form to sop up any excess water that may have accumulated.

Three quick steps: *opening, compressing,* and *sponge-drying.* If you have ever watched potters working on the wheel, these steps are hidden: the potter's hands are at work inside the wall of the vessel. Observers rarely notice this step, and beginners may not realize its importance. And yet, that flat, strong base is key to the stability and usefulness of the final form. Before the potter can continue thinning and shaping the form, there must be a firm foundation.

If you went to Sunday school as a child, you might remember singing about the wise man who built his house upon the rock. "The rain came down and the floods came up, and the house on the rock stood firm."

These song lyrics are taken from one of Jesus' parables. It is recorded twice in the Bible, in Luke 6 and Matthew 7. This short story contrasts wise builders who establish their work on a solid foundation with those who foolishly build upon the sand. Longevity, stability, utility, and safety. All of these depend on a good foundation.

When I was a young Christian, new to my faith, one of my mentors explained that in the Christian life, we should honor Christ by making his life the basis of our own. "How do I do that?" I asked. He tried to make it simple for me; he said, "Time. Treasure. Talent."

TIME: When you look at your schedule, does the way you spend your time reflect Christ as your priority? Does your calendar demonstrate that Christ is more important than any other pursuit?

TREASURE: When you look at your spending habits, does the way you spend your money reflect a commitment to God's kingdom or your own? Does your bank account demonstrate that you put God first?

TALENT: When you consider your unique gifts and talents, does the way you develop and invest them reflect a willingness to love God and serve others? Does your vocation demonstrate a sincere desire to make a difference?

A firm foundation. This step is key to a durable, stable pot. And it is a reminder that we will thrive only if we establish our lives on principles and priorities that endure. Jesus says,

> Everyone who comes to me and hears my words and does them, I will show you what he is like: he is like a man building a house, who dug deep and laid the foundation on the rock. And when a flood arose, the stream broke against that house and could not shake it, because it had been well built. (Luke 6:47–49 ESV)

REFLECTION & DISCUSSION

My mentor encouraged me to take a regular inventory of the ways I was devoting my time, talent, and treasure. He explained that this would help me to build my daily life on a firm foundation.

Can you think of examples in your life that clearly reflect godly priorities?

Is there an area in your life where adjustments (big or small) might make all the difference?

. . .

PRAYER

God, it seems so much easier to say "my life is yours"
and "my heart is yours" than it is to get really specific
and ask whether the way I spend my time, talent,
and treasure reflects heavenly priorities and not
worldly ones. Make me sensitive to the prompting
of your Holy Spirit so that my daily life is truly built
on the solid foundation of things that last. Amen.

STUDIO INSIGHTS

A good base should be flat and sturdy, and roughly the same thickness as the finished walls. Think ahead: leave extra thickness in the base if you plan to trim a *foot ring* into the bottom. Trimming is done when the pot is partially dried, in a state called leather- hard. Keep in mind that it is easy to take clay away, difficult to add it. Start on the thicker side just to be safe.

Uncertain about the thickness of your base as you are throwing? This can be measured by stopping the wheel and grabbing a *needle tool*. Push the tip of the tool straight down into the base until it touches the surface of the wheel or the bat. Then run your finger down along the needle tool until your fingertip touches the base of the pot. Press and hold your finger against the tool and lift the needle tool straight up out of the clay. The distance between the tip of the needle tool and the bottom of your fingertip is the exact thickness of the base.

A note of encouragement: All beginning potters have the experience of opening the cylinder too far, pushing into the center of the clay, and finding that they have pushed straight through the clay and their fingers are scraping against the wheel head. To be honest, even skilled potters get distracted or misjudge their depth and find they've destroyed their base! If you falter, know that you are in good company. Consider it a learning experience, remove the cylinder from the wheel, and start anew.

PULLING

THE POTTER PULLS
THE WALLS INTO
A CYLINDER.

Whether the potter intends to create a mug, vase, pitcher, teapot, planter, or even a bowl, the shaping process starts with a cylinder. This is done through a series of "pulls" that stretch and thin the clay. The short, squat form becomes tall and lean.

Potters begin by adding just enough water so that their hands slide easily over the surface of the clay. The wheel spins at a steady rate. One hand is placed inside the clay form, the other on the outside, and the clay is squeezed in between these two pressure points. Starting at the bottom, the potter applies pressure moving steadily to the top. The pot grows taller, and, in just a few smooth pulls, a thin, straight, cylindrical form is raised.

It takes longer to explain it than to do it! When you watch a master potter pulling the wall of a cylinder and you see the shape transform, it is a dramatic, almost magical step of the process. It looks simple, but beginning potters really struggle here: like first learning to play a musical instrument or drive a car, there seem to be a thousand individual skills to master all at the same time:

- Keep the moisture level right.
- Keep the pressure points of both hands directly opposite one another.
- Move smoothly from the bottom to the top.
- Maintain a consistent pressure.
- Do not make any sudden movements.
- Work carefully in rhythm with the rotation of the wheel.

The key words? *Smooth, steady,* and *consistent.*

So many individual skills to master, but one clear and simple task: using pressure to transform the shapeless lump of clay into a vessel. Notice that it takes the right amount of pressure, applied wisely and consistently, to bring about this astonishing transformation.

Pressure. It seems like such a bad thing, something to be managed or (if possible) to be avoided altogether. The pressure of our busy schedule, the demands of our job, the discomfort of learning a new skill, the expectations we put on ourselves to reach new goals: we resist.

But then again, if we are honest, we recognize that pressure can be a wonderful gift. Pressure turns coal into diamonds. Struggle causes a mollusk to make pearls. What about us? Pressure and struggles motivate us. Think about the way a deadline gets our attention and helps us to devote the necessary effort. The right amount of pressure at the right time can inspire us to meet or exceed our goals. Using the image of the lump of clay, it can push us to grow more, to accomplish more, and—ultimately—to become more.

The right amount of structure and consistent pressure may be exactly what we need to realize our deepest desires, our biggest dreams. We want great things in our lives, and, even though we chafe to acknowledge it, facing challenges and overcoming them may be what it will take to achieve them.

One of the sweetest verses in the Bible, one that specifically uses the image of the potter and the clay, is in the fourth chapter of 2 Corinthians:

> . . . we have this treasure in jars of clay to show that this all-sur-
> passing power is from God and not from us. We are hard pressed
> on every side, but not crushed; perplexed, but not in despair;
> persecuted, but not abandoned; struck down, but not destroyed.
> (2 Corinthians 4:7–9)

Hard-pressed, perplexed, struck down. Disappointed, challenged, struggling. Pulled and stretched. We feel the pressure, inside and out, on a daily basis. I am reminded of the fact that caterpillars must struggle their way out of their cocoons. The struggle is absolutely necessary if they are to fully develop and grow into butterflies.

Athletes lift weights to grow stronger. Students complete tough assignments and are better prepared for their vocation. Apple trees are pruned, and as those newly-trimmed branches are released into the sunlight, they bear more fruit.

For those who love God, who are called according to his purpose, there is reason to hope. The God who made us knows exactly how much pressure is needed to renew and transform us, often making our lives (and hopes and dreams) something larger, taller, and more splendid than we know how to ask or think.

REFLECTION & DISCUSSION

This step is inspiring and dramatic: an unassuming lump of clay is raised from the depths to stand tall and strong; a rather ordinary material suddenly shows that there is more to it than you might expect. Have you seen God work in dramatic ways, transforming a person, a place, or a situation, bringing forth something surprising and wonderful?

Are there challenges you are currently facing, things you really don't want to deal with or truly do not want to do, that might possibly be part of God's training program to help you grow? What would it look like for you to get in step with the way God is growing you so that you are equipped to meet the challenges that the future may bring?

. . .

PRAYER

Father God, I have been told that you are good and that your plans for me are "to give me a future and a hope" (Jer. 29:11). I sort of believe that. I do. Now show me what the next steps are for me to see you as you really are and grow in faith and trust. As I consider the future, awaken new dreams, and grant me new courage. I am asking that I may trust your wisdom and your ability to use the challenges of this season of life to bring about something bigger and better than I could ever accomplish in my own strength. Amen.

STUDIO INSIGHTS

Pulling the walls of a cylinder looks and feels like magic! The wheel is spinning more slowly as you place one hand on the outside and one on the inside. Position your fingertips opposite one another. Starting at the bottom of the cylinder, put pressure on the clay wall and slowly move up, from the bottom to the top. You are squeezing the clay between the pressure points produced by your fingertips. It's tempting to pinch your fingers tighter and tighter as you go, but hold them steady and move the clay up into even walls. And don't forget to BREATHE!

As with other steps in the pottery-making process, you should experiment with different approaches and see what gives you the best control. Many potters prefer to use their knuckles rather than their fingers to create the right pressure points and achieve a smooth, strong, effective pull. Experiment. Watching other potters at work, in your studio or through online videos, will help you picture the process and may offer insight into different ways to approach this step.

One secret is learning to move in rhythm with the turning wheel. Picture the cylinder completing one full rotation as you squeeze the clay and move your hands upward bit by bit. As you pull up, the clay wall gets thinner and the cylinder gets taller, forming a straight, even wall.

The goal of pulling is to distribute all of the available clay evenly from the bottom of the cylinder to the very top. New potters tend to be a bit timid about the amount of pressure they place at the bottom of their cylinders, right where the bottom of the wall meets the base of the pot. But this is exactly where extra clay can accumulate, resulting in a vessel that is unbalanced and clunky, needs significant trimming, or splits and breaks in the heat of firing.

RECLAIMING

IF THE CLAY WEAKENS, WOBBLES, AND COLLAPSES, GOD IS NOT DAUNTED

The Old Testament prophets really had it rough.

What about poor Ezekiel? Has to draw a picture of Jerusalem and then lie down on his left side for 390 days. And then bake bread out of wheat, barley, beans, lentils, millet, and spelt and cook it over cow dung (Ezek. 4).

What about poor Ahijah? Buys a brand-new cloak and then God tells him to tear it into twelve pieces and start handing them out (1 Kings 11:29–39).

What about poor Jeremiah? Buries his new linen belt in the dirt (Jer. 13). Gets tossed in a cistern (Jer. 38). Has a vision: not of heavenly angels, but of rotten figs (Jer. 24).

God constantly uses vivid pictures to teach his people spiritual lessons. So God talks to the prophet Jeremiah about potters and clay. God tells him to go down to the potter's house, "and there I will give you my message" (Jer. 18:2).

Jeremiah obeys. He watches the potter working on the wheel, and as we have seen, many things about this experience are vivid, powerful, and relevant to the human experience. But this time, as Jeremiah watches the potter and the clay, something goes terribly wrong:

> The pot he was shaping from the clay was marred in his hands.
> (Jeremiah 18:4)

What went wrong? What would cause a pot to become marred in the hands of the potter? It could be that one of those impurities, one of those bumps or bubbles, came to the surface and knocked things off center.

It could be that one of those wobbles, so tiny at the centering stage, became bigger and bigger until the whole thing started to lean and warp and then toppled right over.

Let's assume that the clay was clean, the centering was done correctly, and the potter was both skillful and careful. Even with all of that going for it, the pot still may be marred. There are lots of things that can cause it, but one of the most common causes of damage at this point is called "clay fatigue." That's right, fatigue. As the clay is pulled and stretched, the structure of the clay can become overwhelmed.

Ever felt like you've been pulled one time too many and simply flopped right over? Ever had one of those days?

Here is the good news. If the pot becomes marred at this point in the process, it is fairly easy for the potter to reclaim it.

The clay is still moist, soft, and resilient. The clay is taken off the wheel and excess moisture is removed. Then the clay can be wedged, patted into shape, and reattached to the wheel. The potter sets the wheel to spinning and simply starts centering, opening, and pulling all over again.

When the pot is overwhelmed and everything comes tumbling down, it may seem like a disaster, but the potter is never daunted. There is always something he can do.

REFLECTION & DISCUSSION

Fatigue is a fact of life for most of us. Consider if there is a need in your life right now to make changes that will bring refreshment and prevent the destruction of mind and body that comes from accumulated fatigue. Then consider: Is there someone you know who is facing serious challenges in the push and pull of life? Is there something you (or your small group) can do this week to reduce the stress and help carry the load?

Think of a time when you have faced a major setback—when things did not go smoothly, when the process was interrupted by an unexpected collapse. Do you have a testimony of the way that God moved into that situation and made things right?

PRAYER

Identify one particular situation that seems beyond repair. Then pray:

Lord, I just can't see how this situation
could possibly be reclaimed. Give me
the strength to scoop up this soggy mess,
put it in your loving hands, and trust you
to make it right again. Amen.

STUDIO INSIGHTS

What can go wrong in the shaping process? Here are some factors to consider.

Wrong wheel speed: Centering works best at a higher speed; opening and pulling works best at a slower speed. The speed of the wheel may need to be adjusted for other reasons, such as the amount of clay you are using, or the nature of the clay body.

Movements that are out of sync: It takes practice to work evenly from bottom to top in tandem with the spinning wheel. Pay close attention to your throwing lines: if there is equal spacing between each row, you will know that you're moving at a consistent speed.

Uneven pressure: When you are working with one hand inside the cylinder and the other on the outside, it is easy for your pressure points to be misaligned, with one hand sliding higher than the other. Keep your fingers (or knuckles) opposite each other, squeezing the clay in between.

Abrupt motion: Clay is a marvelous medium to work with because it responds so quickly to the movements of your hands. This is the result of plasticity, the way that clay can be stretched and shaped and then hold its form. But be careful: pressing suddenly or releasing pressure abruptly can throw your work off-center. And do not touch the clay unless the wheel is in motion.

Clay fatigue: When clay is overworked, it absorbs too much water, and this weakens the walls. Fine-textured clays like porcelain are particularly prone to this.

Until clay is fired, it can be remixed, re-wedged, and reused an infinite number of times. That's why every potter has a process for gathering, processing, and reclaiming used clay. What a joy it is to know that hidden within the slop and slip of a reclaim bucket, there are beautiful and useful pots just waiting to be brought to life again in the hands of the potter.

X

SHAPING

THE POTTER USES PRESSURE,

INSIDE AND OUT,

TO SHAPE THE CLAY.

Now it's time for the fancy stuff. This is what we've been waiting for. Every step before this one is preparation; every step after is finishing work. This is the moment of truth. The potter starts working on the cylinder section by section to give it shape. The bottom, or foot, of the pot may be wide or narrow, straight or slanted. The sides, or walls, form the main part of the pot: the potter may push out to create a rounded form or press in to narrow it. The potter shapes the shoulder, or upper section, and the neck, the top section. Finally, he or she will decide upon a finish for the edge, which is called the lip. Sometimes pressure is firm redirection and at other times gentle beckoning, but always for the growth and good of the piece.

Each pot is shaped according to the potter's will. One day, I might make coffee mugs, cereal bowls, teapots, or mixing bowls because I need something useful for my kitchen. Another day, I might make a slender vase because I need something beautiful for my living room. From time to time, the qualities of a particular clay body suggest its own purpose: a delicate porcelain becomes a translucent teacup. Hearty red earthenware becomes a faceted flowerpot. Brown stoneware is perfect for a lantern, pierced to let candlelight shine through.

Whether I am creating a pot because there is a need for something to function in my household or a need for beauty somewhere in my world, a need to express the joy of creativity or a need to respond sensitively to the materials at hand, I make each pot as I see fit.

And as I work, good clay doesn't argue. In Isaiah 45:9, it says:

> Woe to those who quarrel with their Maker ... Does the clay say to the potter, "What are you making?"

Do we do that? When God is making choices and issuing directions, do we dig in our heels and say, "Hey! Wait a minute! Exactly what do you think you are doing?"

You want me to do what? Gosh, Lord, you don't mean it. Don't you remember what happened last time I tried that? I mean really ...

You want me to talk to who? Surely, Lord, you don't mean it. Don't you remember what they did to me last week? After all ...

You want me to go where? No, that can't possibly be right. Are you sure you know what you're talking about? Think about it this way ...

You wanted that done when? If only you understood, Lord, how inconvenient your timing is. You really have to consider ...

I have heard that you can say "no" or you can say "Lord," but you cannot say "No, Lord," and mean it. It's one or the other. Either God is our Lord and we say yes to his will in his time in his way, or he is not Lord, and we say no to what he is calling us to.

Jonah was given a very clear command to go to Nineveh and preach good news (Jonah 1:2). He heard exactly what God told him, and he understood it unequivocally. And he ran the other way.

Ananias, on the other hand, responded righteously. In Acts 9:10–11, we are told that God came to him with a very clear command to go to Damascus and speak good news:

> There was a disciple named Ananias. The Lord called to him
> in a vision,
> "Ananias!"
> "Yes, Lord," he answered.
> The Lord told him, "Go to the house of Judas on Straight Street
> and ask for a man from Tarsus named Saul, for he is praying. In
> a vision he has seen a man named Ananias come and place his
> hands on him to restore his sight." (Acts 9:10–11)

House of Judas. Okay. Straight Street. Okay. Laying on of hands. Okay. Restore his sight. Sounds good. Um, wait a minute, Lord. Did you say Saul of Tarsus?

The next scene is one of my favorites in all of Scripture. Ananias is one of my heroes of the faith—I relate to him more than I relate to most other Bible characters. That's because most of the time, I am not like Jonah, seized by fear and quick to flee in the opposite direction. But I am not like Samuel, either, who hears God and quietly says, "Speak, for your servant is listening" (1 Sam. 3:7–10). Or the prophet Isaiah, who hears God and instantly responds, "Here I am. Send me" (Isa. 6:8).

Instead, I am a lot like Ananias. I love God and hear God and, a lot of the time, I need a little help to sort it out and get it right. There is a difference between arguing with God and talking things out. When God tells him to go and pray for Saul of Tarsus, Ananias thinks that maybe God is a little bit confused and needs a few things pointed out to him:

> "Lord," Ananias answered, "I have heard many reports about this man and all the harm he has done to your saints in Jerusalem. And he has come here with authority from the chief priests to arrest all who call on your name." (Acts 9:13–14)

Listen, God. Haven't you been following the news? Didn't you read the latest *Jerusalem Post*? This Saul character? He's a bad one. This is a foolish thing you are calling me to do! Are you sure you know what you are asking?

I don't think Ananias is being resistant. I don't think he is being disobedient. After all, he prefaces his words with the declaration LORD. This command just doesn't make sense to him, and so he wants to clarify things, wants to be sure. Mary does the same thing when the angel announces that she will be the mother of the Messiah: I am available, she says, but I really don't understand. Please, can you explain how this thing is going to work?

God answers honest questions and honors those who seek him by addressing their concerns.

> But the Lord said to Ananias, "Go! This man is my chosen instrument to proclaim my name to the Gentiles and their kings and to the people of Israel." Then God adds, "I will show him how much he must suffer for my name." (Acts 9:15–16)

So Ananias went.

We don't always know why God shapes one person one way and another person another way. Why life takes a turn in an unexpected direction, why plans go awry, or why a goal is thwarted. I believe that God loves to take the time to talk with us about those things that are troubling our hearts. But here's the catch: he is still Lord. He may graciously take the time to reason with us. He may explain things with great clarity and purpose. Or he may be stubbornly silent on the matter. In either case, at some point or another, he will say, "Go!" And that's exactly what we must do.

REFLECTION & DISCUSSION

Think about the shape of your past. Is there an unexpected turn of events that didn't make sense at the time but now is a clear indication of God's good and perfect will? Share that story with someone this week. It will be an encouragement to them and to you.

Think about the shape of your future. In your heart, are you clear about saying an unconditional "Yes!" to Jesus, the Lord? If you sense a place of resistance, ask for God's help to identify it, understand it, and work through it.

.   .   .

PRAYER

Lord, forgive me for all of the times
that I have argued, explained, excused, and
fought the shaping process in my life.
I really do want the shape of my life to reflect
your good and perfect will. I really want the shape
of my soul to reflect the character and nature of Jesus.
Sometimes, I'm not very good at saying "Yes, Lord."
But I want to get better at it.
So let me make this declaration now.
If you want to make my life into something that is useful
to your kingdom, take me. In the past, I've said no,
maybe, later, we'll see. Today I say, "Yes, Lord."
And tomorrow when I wake,
pour out a fresh batch of grace so that I have
all that I need to say "Yes, Lord," again and again.
Thank you for loving me enough to keep forming
and shaping and molding and working in
my life, day by day by day. Amen.

STUDIO INSIGHTS

Shaping is the result of varying the pressure as you squeeze the clay wall from bottom to top. Potters push from the inside to "belly out" the wall and make the pot wider. They press inward to create a taller, more narrow shape. Or they apply pressure with both hands on the outside of the pot and "collar in" to shape the neck of a vase.

You can use a number of different tools to aid in this shaping process. A flat tool called a *rib* can help guide the form you are trying to achieve. Some ribs are curved. Others are notched. These not only give shape to a vessel. Ribs strengthen the wall because they remove excess water from the surface and compress the clay to keep it strong. They can also add texture or be used to scratch a design into the pot's surface.

A needle tool can trim excess clay from the lip or from the bottom of the pot. As we have seen, it can also help you measure the thickness of your base. It also comes in handy if the top edge of your pot gets wonky: trim away the excess, and continue to pull, shape, or smooth.

Pottery sponges come in a variety of shapes and thicknesses. Every experienced potter I know has a favorite, well-worn sponge. They are used to smooth the surface or control moisture or to create a wider, flatter surface at a pressure point.

There are also a wide variety of *modeling tools* that may be used to modify the shape or add texture and interest to the surface of the clay.

Pottery-making is a hands-on process, but don't forget that many tools are available to expand the creative possibilities. And don't hesitate to create new pottery tools from items in your home or objects found in nature. These add beautiful variety to your work as you shape and finish your piece.

REFINING

THE POTTER TRIMS
AND REFINES THE CLAY.

The clay has been found, cleaned, and wedged then opened, pulled, and shaped. Once shaping is complete and the vessel is fully formed, the potter removes it from the wheel. We're done now. Or so it seems . . .

In fact, the potter may continue the creative process while the clay is still soft and resilient. The rim of the pot might be stretched outward to make a spout for a large water pitcher or a small crock for cream. A handle (or pair of handles) may be pulled, shaped, and attached. Decorative elements such as coils or slabs may be added. Potters can create stunning pieces--large, complex, asymmetrical, and inventive by manipulating the clay.

At this point, potters often sign their name to the bottom of the piece or add a *maker's mark* (sometimes called a *chop mark*): a stamp that is pressed into the bottom or the side of the pot. This identifies the artist and marks the clay piece as their own.

And now the pot is set aside to dry. As water evaporates, the clay shrinks. The structure becomes stiff and solid: now the vessel can be handled without losing its shape. At this stage, the clay is said to be *leather-hard*. This can take only a few hours in an arid climate; if the weather is stormy or humidity is high, it can take several days.

The leather-hard stage opens a world of possibilities! Simple forms become complex by adding decorative elements. Plain forms gain interest through thoughtful design. A basic cylinder, bowl, or vase can take on a whole new identity as segments are joined together: a handle is added, for example, or two or three thrown forms are combined into one.

But the most common work for the leather-hard vessel is trimming, sometimes called *turning*. The potter returns to the potter's wheel. The pot is carefully centered and attached to the wheel, the wheel is set to rotate very slowly, and the potter carves away clay.

Clay may be removed to refine the shape of the pot and even out the thickness of the walls. During this step, a good potter is sensitive and careful, because it's all too easy to trim too far. You might see a good potter stop from time to time and tap on the piece in different places. They can tell by the sound which areas are too thick and where it is safe to continue trimming away.

The very best pots are perfectly even the whole way through. They feel balanced and light in your hands, almost like they are going to float away. The proportions are balanced, and the form is graceful.

Finally, the potter will attend to the small details, taking special care with the foot of the pot. The bottom surface may be designed to be smooth and straight, or the potter may carve out the clay from the center of the foot to create a *foot ring*. A damp sponge is used to clean and finish the base.

When I attend an art sale, say at a gallery or street fair, I can always tell which shoppers are knowledgeable about pottery. Most people walk by the displays and look at the pots. But the artists? They will pick up the pot and and weigh it in their hands. Then they turn it upside down. They are looking for a signature. They are checking the weight and the balance. They are also examining the finishing work, the evidence of careful craftsmanship. They know that a seasoned potter takes extra care not only with the top and the sides but also with the intentional design and careful finish of the bottom of the vessel.

This kind of care should be a hallmark of our character, too.

We should be faithful in the small things. As it says in Luke 16:10: "Whoever can be trusted with very little can also be trusted with much."

We should be faithful in the hidden things. As it says in Mark 4:22: "For nothing is hidden except to be made manifest, nor is anything secret except to come to light." (ESV)

We should be faithful to persist, from the beginning to the very end, as it says in Matthew 24:13, Romans 5, and James 5:11. As it promises in Galatians 6:9: "Let's not get tired of doing what is good. At just the right time we will reap a harvest of blessing if we don't give up." (NLT)

Through the process, we find strength in knowing that, like a careful potter, God has begun a good work, and he will be faithful to complete it.

REFLECTION & DISCUSSION

No doubt you have cups, vases, and other vessels in your home, and chances are, you've never flipped them over and examined the bottom of these pieces. Try it. Then consider: Might it be useful to take a look underneath persistent problem areas of our lives? Might a new point of view lead to new insights and breakthroughs?

PRAYER

Heavenly Father, I understand that
the clay pot reaches its full potential
when the refining and finishing work
is thorough, careful, and complete.
Help my life and my character
to be continually, persistently shaped
to reflect your character, according to
your good plans for me. Amen.

STUDIO INSIGHTS

When trimming a pot, a variety of tools are used to refine the shape and carve out a foot ring. This step of careful finishing is a hallmark of good potters. But trimming is not the only option when working with leather-hard clay. Consider the creative opportunities of these techniques:

Adding: The coffee mug I am using today is made of two pieces: a cylinder and a handle. A teapot is made of four distinct sections: the body, the handle, a spout, and a lid. Mugs and teapots are examples of *composite* forms. The various pieces are created separately and then joined together when leather-hard. The connection points are scored by scratching the connection points with a needle tool and then slip is applied. Pieces are pressed together and edges refined. Joining pieces may be used to create functional work. Joining may also be a way to create large, extravagant pieces, unusual shapes, or combinations of sculpture with thrown ware.

Burnishing: A wooden rib or other tool is used to polish the surface, compressing the clay and leaving it smooth and shiny. Native American pottery often uses this technique.

Coloring with slip: Liquid clay called *slip* can be painted on the surface.

Faceting: A *fettling knife* or taut wire can be used to slice clay from the surface to create flat planes that form a pleasing pattern. This can be done over one small part of the surface or all of it, and the final effect can add interest and beauty to the finished work.

Incising: Surface decoration can be added by scratching or carving lines into the pottery, creating a pattern, drawing a picture, or producing a simple or complex design.

Piercing: Clay that is leather-hard is stable enough to be cut straight through to create openings. These may serve as design elements or be used to create a candle holder that lets light shine through.

P E R S I S T I N G

THE LEATHER-HARD POT
IS LEFT ALONE UNTIL
IT IS BONE DRY.

Once the shaping and trimming processes are complete, the pot is set aside to dry. After enduring so much pressure and experiencing such close, careful attention from the potter, now all of a sudden the pot is set aside and left alone. Pressure and pulling are uncomfortable, but what is this sudden isolation, sudden stillness? Left alone on the shelf, away from the hurry and the noise. Have I been abandoned? Have I been rejected? Did I do something wrong? Is this the end of my story?

It is like the forty days that Jesus spent in the wilderness early in his ministry. When we remember this story, we don't actually think much about the forty days at all. In our minds, we tend to go immediately to day forty-one. Satan appears and presents the Lord with three temptations. Jesus overcomes each one by quoting Scripture. Man does not live by bread alone! Worship the Lord God and serve him only! Do not put the Lord God to the test! (Luke 4:1–13) It is dramatic. Christ is triumphant. And it is the climactic event that launches him into public ministry.

But what about that period of forty long days? Forty days. That's more than a month without food, without friends. What was happening in that desert time? Didn't the hours seem awfully long? Wasn't the pace awfully slow? Weren't his patience and his persistence tested day after day, long before the devil arrived on the scene? And in some ways, weren't those days of testing just as difficult simply because they were not nearly so dramatic?

What is both hard to remember and important to understand is that times of waiting are not accidental. God's timing is not tardy, his purpose is not lost, his work is not abandoned, his promise is not forgotten. The great saints have always faced times when they wondered and waited. Abraham and Sarai sitting childless in their tent. Joseph languishing in Pharaoh's prison. Moses tending sheep in the desert for more than forty years. Ruth gleaning in the fields day after day after day. Nehemiah worrying about the condition of Jerusalem's walls.

Even King David: David was still a teenager when the prophet Samuel anointed him to be Israel's next king. It is a dramatic moment, told in 1 Samuel 16. And after that? David went back to tending sheep. He refused to take matters into his own hands to expedite his kingship, waiting for God to bring it to pass. David was thirty years old when he finally (finally!) began his reign (2 Sam. 5:4).

Waiting. Not much going on. Hope once burned bright, but now? Now it's all ashes and wondering.

But God has not forgotten.

The Lord is not slow in keeping his promise, as some understand slowness. Instead he is patient with you . . . (2 Peter 3:9)

The example of the clay makes this clear. The potter has not forgotten the pot. The pot has been set aside on purpose, that a particular work be accomplished. Through sitting and waiting. This period of persistence is absolutely necessary. The pot must dry completely, top to bottom, through and through. If moisture is hidden in the wall of the pot, there will be trouble when the pot is fired. That is because water heats up much faster than clay. As the kiln gets hotter, any remaining water will turn to steam and explode out of the side of the pot. Impatience brings disaster: the pot will shatter.

That's why the pot is left to sit and wait until it is absolutely dry. It is brought to a state known as bone dry.

Waiting. Sitting. Silent. Untouched. Unnoticed. Persisting until the work is thoroughly finished. Patience, too, is a necessary part of the process.

REFLECTION & DISCUSSION

Is there a time in your life when a project has been ruined or compromised because you were impatient and skipped some steps along the way? Ask God to forgive you, and then ask him to show you what you might learn from the experience.

Is there a particular project or event or issue in your life right now that seems to be on hold? Find someone to pray with this week and seek God's direction concerning it. With the help of a trusted friend, seek to discern if now is the time for things to change, or if this is a time to wait. Patiently. For the fullness of time. Until this stage of the process is truly completed.

PRAYER

God, I do not like to sit and wait.
I don't really trust the dry times
when nothing seems to be happening.
Help me to grow in trust and patience
so that I can understand what John Milton
meant when he wrote, "They also serve
who only stand and wait." Amen.

STUDIO INSIGHTS

There is much you *can't* do with clay at the bone-dry stage because it's so fragile. But if you are careful, this can be the ideal time to add surface decoration.

Metallic Oxides: An oxide wash is a suspension of metallic powder that can be brushed on a bone-dry or bisque-fried pot. Designs may be freehand, geometric, or representational, such as flowers or animals. Different colors can be achieved by different oxides. Chrome will fire green. Manganese is brown. Copper is unpredictable and may turn aqua, green, or even pink. Oxides can be toxic and should be handled with care.

Underglazes: An underglaze is a creamy mixture of clay with colorants. It is brushed onto the surface of a bone-dry or bisque-fired pot and often covered with a clear or translucent glaze. The result is a surface design with depth and richness.

Image transfers: Pictures can be transferred to a pot's surface: First, images are drawn or traced onto paper, and then transfer templates are created.

Water etching: This technique can produce truly remarkable effects. Begin by drawing a design on the pot with a pencil and then brush shellac, Mod Podge, or wax on the parts of the design that you want to appear raised. Now, take a damp sponge and wipe over the surface of the pot. The water will remove clay that is not covered by the wax and leave raised designs. The wax and pencil lines will burn off in the kiln.

Keep imagining the possibilities for surface design on the vessels you create. The possibilities are vast, and the results are truly remarkable.

RESTORING

IF THE BONE-DRY POT IS CHIPPED, CRACKED, OR DROPPED, GOD IS NOT DAUNTED.

During this dry time, the pot is extremely vulnerable: even gentle handling can cause chips, splits, and cracks. This lesson really came into focus for me as I worked with Adam, the photographer whose work is featured in the first edition of this book. He watched me select and prepare the clay. He took pictures as I centered, opened, pulled, and shaped several pots. And he handled all kinds of pots, pots that I had made, and pots made by others.

In particular, he took several pictures of a large, beautiful vase made by Susan Ney. The pot was bone dry.

There was only one problem: he didn't know it was bone dry. He thought it had already been fired. As we finished the photo shoot and started cleaning up, he grabbed this beautiful vase by the inside of the lip and swung around to take it back to its shelf inside the studio.

That vase crumbled to pieces in his hand. I walked by just seconds after it happened—his eyes were wide, and the broken bits covered the ground around his feet. "I—I don't understand. I was so careful . . ." he started. And that's true. He had been careful. Very careful. But that pot was bone dry. Even the most careful handling at this point can cause everything to fall to pieces.

Here is the good news. If the pot becomes marred at this point in the process, it is still possible for the potter to make things right.

If the break is small, the pot can be patched and repaired. A chipped lip can be sanded and smoothed. A bumped handle can be reattached.

If the damage is extensive, the restoration process takes longer. The broken bits are gathered together and soaked in water (remember that water is a picture of the Holy Spirit). The clay dissolves and returns to its soft, resilient state. Then the clay is wedged and reattached to the wheel head. And the potter starts the centering and shaping process all over again.

A good potter can make that same pot all over again. A very good potter can make something even better. Better? Yes, better. God can pick up the broken pieces of our lives, our ministries, our hearts, our hopes, our dreams. He can saturate them in the power of the Holy Spirit. Those broken pieces become soft, resilient, and pliable, just like they used to be. And God, the Master Potter, can make that very same pot all over again. Or maybe, just maybe, he will not only restore them: he will make something even better.

When we understand this principle, we see that bone-dry pots can be transformed and given new life. It is like another powerful picture, one that God gave to the prophet Ezekiel:

> The hand of the Lord was upon me, and he brought me out by the Spirit of the Lord and set me in the middle of a valley; it was full of bones. He led me back and forth among them, and I saw a great many bones on the floor of the valley, bones that were very dry.

He asked me, "Son of man, can these bones live?"

I said, "O Sovereign Lord, you alone know."

Then he said to me, "Prophesy to these bones and say to them, 'Dry bones, hear the word of the Lord! This is what the Sovereign Lord says to these bones: I will make breath enter you, and you will come to life. I will attach tendons to you and make flesh come upon you and cover you with skin; I will put breath in you, and you will come to life. Then you will know that I am the Lord.'"

So I prophesied as I was commanded. And as I was prophesying, there was a noise, a rattling sound, and the bones came together, bone to bone. I looked, and tendons and flesh appeared on them and skin covered them, but there was no breath in them.

Then he said to me, "Prophesy to the breath; prophesy, son of man, and say to it, 'This is what the Sovereign Lord says: Come, breath, from the four winds, and breathe into these slain, that they may live.'"

So I prophesied as he commanded me, and breath entered them; they came to life. (Ezekiel 37:1–10)

New life for old. It is one of the most powerful pictures in the Bible. It is one of the most beautiful promises of God. It is available for you.

REFLECTION & DISCUSSION

Do you have broken pieces of some situation, some life dream, some relationship, some gift or ability that seems broken beyond repair? Give the pieces to God in prayer—and see what he will do.

When my photographer broke that pot, he went to the potter and quickly apologized and offered to make restitution. She responded graciously, with strong words of forgiveness and encouragement. Is there something you have broken but have not yet made right—a promise, a commitment, perhaps a possession? Even when we are being very careful, our words and actions can be destructive, and we need to do everything in our power to make things right. Are there things that you need to do this week to make amends?

. . .

PRAYER

For this prayer time, let me pray this prayer over you:

Sovereign Lord, in the life and heart
of this precious one, there are disappointments
and injuries of every kind. There are dreams
that have died. There are people who have been lost.
There are relationships broken. There are hopes dashed.
There are longings that remain unfulfilled.
O God, let these bones live. Restore, revive, refresh.
Breathe on them, Breath of Life. Give them hope.
Make them new. Amen.

STUDIO INSIGHTS

Whether at work in an individual studio or a busy classroom, potters have many different ways to reclaim and reuse clay. As we have seen, the process starts with a reclaim bucket: scraps, slop, slip, practice pieces, trimmings, lugs, and other bits of unwanted, unfired clay are gathered into large plastic buckets or bins. The clay is covered with water and left to sit.

Once the clay has completely dissolved, it can be scooped out and spread on a large plaster slab. This draws out excess moisture. A little time and patience, and then it is ready to be wedged in small batches and used again.

Some studios invest in a specially designed machine called a pugmill. A pugmill mixes used clay into a homogeneous state. It removes all the air bubbles and then extrudes the soft, smooth, workable clay. The clay can then be gathered into large plastic bags, ready to be used.

Larger, more powerful pugmills have many different industrial uses. You can find them producing mineral mixtures for a road base, mixing concrete, or preparing a consistent mineral mixture for landfill. But in the artist's studio, a pugmill transforms scraps into workable clay that has exactly the right consistency. Even clay that has been dried out or become too stiff to work with can be rehydrated and then remixed in a pugmill and made as good as new.

TRANSFORMING

THE POT IS PLACED INTO
THE KILN AND FIRED.

As the pot waits and dries, it must be tedious and tiresome, at least at first. But if all goes well, I wonder if that pot doesn't settle in and get pretty comfortable. It is nice and quiet, after all. The potter seems to have gone off somewhere and left the pot to its own devices. So maybe the pot figures that since it's been left to fend for itself, it'll just make the best of it.

The owner of the vineyard leaves, and the tenants are left to steward the property (Mark 12:1–12).

The master goes on a journey, and the workers are entrusted with the careful use of their talents (Matt. 25:14–30).

The bridegroom is delayed, and those waiting for him are expected to keep their lamps trim and bright (Matt. 25:1–13).

But after a while, the tenants start to get selfish, the workers start to get lazy, and the young girls get a little sleepy. Luke warns us that we are wise to keep watch and stay ready.

> It will be good for those servants whose master finds them
> watching when he comes. (Luke 12:37)

Waiting patiently is one thing. Waiting expectantly, alert, and prepared is even better.

Because suddenly, without warning, time's up.

The potter picks the pot up off the shelf and stacks it in a kiln. The kiln may be large or small. It may be powered by gas, electricity, or wood.

No matter its size or kind, the purpose of the kiln is to heat the pot to nearly 2,000°F. The firing process heats the clay so hot that a complete transformation takes place. The clay becomes very hard. Heat rises, and the clay goes through a process called "sintering." As the bond between particles is strengthened, the pot becomes harder and more compact. After it is fired, the pot is smaller, lighter, and much, much stronger. Fired clay is permanent: it will no longer dissolve in water.

It is interesting to me that pots are shaped alone on the potter's wheel, but most often, they go through the fire together. After drying, the pots are stacked on top of one another and crowded together. In a similar way, God often gives us companions in the fiery trials of life, companions who can pray with us, talk with us, and stand with us.

That was the case with Shadrach, Meshach, and Abednego. We read in the third chapter of Daniel that Nebuchadnezzar became furious with Shadrach, Meshach, and Abednego because they refused to bow down to the idol he had made. So the king took action:

> He ordered the furnace heated seven times hotter than usual
> and commanded some of the strongest soldiers in his army to tie
> up Shadrach, Meshach and Abednego and throw them into the
> blazing furnace. (Daniel 3:19–20)

We have looked at difficult times in the process of making a pot. The pot is cleaned, wedged, stretched, and dried. Now comes the very worst of it: the pot is flung into the blazing furnace. Hot. Very hot. Impossibly hot.

> The king's command was so urgent and the furnace so hot that
> the flames of the fire killed the men who took up Shadrach,
> Meshach and Abednego, and these three men, firmly tied, fell
> into the blazing furnace. (Daniel 3:22–23)

The fire is hot and the fire is dangerous. It can bring about great harm. But although our enemies, and the Enemy of our Souls, may intend the fire for great harm, our God is able to use it to bring about great good.

The one who is tested comes forth as fine gold (Job 23:10).

The one who is pruned bears much fruit (John 15:2).

The pot that is fired is made strong and useful.

Think about it. If I put hot coffee or cold milk or ice water into an unfired clay vessel, the whole thing will dissolve into a big old pile of mush. It hasn't been tested, hasn't been tried. It hasn't been made strong in the fire. So, while it may look very attractive, it really can't be used. It's not good for anything. Not until it is transformed by fire.

The process of transforming isn't easy, and it isn't comfortable. But one thing we can count on is that Christ will meet us in the midst of it all. Think again of Shadrach, Meshach, and Abednego in the fire:

King Nebuchadnezzar leaped to his feet in amazement and asked his advisors, "Weren't there three men that we tied up and threw into the fire?"

They replied, "Certainly, Your Majesty."

He said, "Look! I see four men walking around in the fire, unbound and unharmed, and the fourth looks like a son of the gods."

Nebuchadnezzar then approached the opening of the blazing furnace and shouted, "Shadrach, Meshach and Abednego, servants of the Most High God, come out! Come here!"

So Shadrach, Meshach and Abednego came out of the fire, and the satraps, prefects, governors and royal advisers crowded around them. They saw that the fire had not harmed their bodies, nor was a hair of their heads singed; their robes were not scorched, and there was no smell of fire on them.

Then Nebuchadnezzar said, "Praise be to the God of Shadrach, Meshach and Abednego, who has sent his angel and rescued his servants! They trusted in him and defied the king's command and were willing to give up their lives rather than serve or worship any god except their own God." (Daniel 3:24–28)

Praise be to the God of Shadrach, Meshach, and Abednego! Nebuchadnezzar saw it clearly: "No other God can save in this way" (3:29). The fire is hot and the trial is hard. But in the end, God is glorified and God's people are made strong.

How should we respond when fiery trials come? I don't much like the answer. But here it is, straight from the book of James:

Consider it pure joy, my brothers and sisters, whenever you face trials of many kinds, because you know that the testing of your faith produces perseverance. Let perseverance finish its work so that you may be mature and complete, not lacking anything. (James 1:2–4)

REFLECTION & DISCUSSION

What does it mean to you to be prepared for whatever trials may come? What spiritual rhythms do you have in place that help prepare you for the unexpected trials of life?

Thank God for those who have stood by your side during fiery trials. Then thank them: Take time this week to send a text or write a note or make a call saying thank you to someone who has stood by you in tough times.

PRAYER

Dear God, consider my trials pure joy?
Hmmm. I'm not there quite yet. But I'm learning, Lord,
to accept good times and bad times as gifts from your hand.
I'm learning to ask, "What is God saying to me in the
midst of this circumstance?" And I'm starting to see that
these things happen for a reason, that they can help
to accomplish important things in my life. I am persuaded
that no matter how hot the fire gets, you mean it when you
say that you will *never* leave me, you will *never* forsake me.
I'm learning, Lord. Help me to understand it better.
Help me to live it more. Amen.

STUDIO INSIGHTS

Whether raw clay is liquid (*slip* or *slurry*), solid (*leather-hard* and cool to the touch), or dry as a bone, it can be worked and reworked over and over again. But once clay has been fired, a chemical transformation takes place: clay becomes ceramic.

The first time through the kiln is called a *bisque* firing. As the temperature, rises, any remaining moisture evaporates from the clay body. Next, organic binders within the clay, like plant fibers, are burned away. Finally, chemically-bound water molecules are driven off and the clay particles fuse, creating a rock-solid, permanent bond. The bisque-fired pot is hard, porous, and smaller: clay shrinks as this chemical process takes place. It no longer dissolves in water.

There is an art to working with clay; there is also an art to firing the kiln. The kiln does have a series of gauges (called a thermocouple) that indicate the interior temperature as pots are being fired, but most studios measure the firing temperature more precisely by using *pyrometric cones.* These are small, tall, triangles made of glaze along with an added *flux,* or melting agent. Each cone is formulated to bend at specific temperatures over a specific amount of time. You'll hear potters talk about "Cone 10" or "Cone 6" or "Cone 04" firings.

In fact, cones don't just measure temperature; they indicate what is called "heatwork," which is the effect of temperature on the clay as it is fired. Temperature, time, and even how fast the temperature is raised inside the kiln will affect the melting point of a cone. Cones communicate the precise conditions within the kiln and give the potter the details they need to guide and tend these particular works of art.

XVI

RETURNING

THE POT IS GLAZED AND
GOES BACK INTO THE FIRE.

Several years ago, I bought a small house, the kind that is called a "fixer-upper." It was tiny and shabby and adorable. I couldn't wait to begin the transformation process, to roll up my sleeves, and see how God might make a mountain of glory out of this little molehill. Two days after I moved in, I headed for the backyard with my toolbox in hand. The first job was to scrape off the years of grime and old paint from the windows and let the sun shine through. So I grabbed a razor tool in my right hand.

But I grabbed it too quickly, too carelessly. It slipped, and the corner of the blade slid into the knuckle of my little finger. The wound was quick and very deep.

The orthopedic surgeon told me that I had completely severed my tendon, and he would have to open up my hand to reattach it. He rushed me to the hospital, and as I waited in the prep room, the anesthesiologist and nurse sat with me and told me about the procedure. I was relaxed, even cheerful. They seemed puzzled by that, but the explanation was simple: I had never had any kind of surgery before. I had never even been hospitalized before. I had no idea what I was in for.

If I had to return to the hospital and go through surgery again, knowing what I know now about how difficult and painful it is—the months of recovery, the difficulty of physical therapy, the disfiguring effect of that long, pink scar—I might not be so cavalier about it all. I was brave only because I had no idea how hard it would be.

Clay that has never been fired is a little bit like that. The potter lifts the pot and loads it into the kiln. The clay has absolutely no idea what it is in for. To say yes to the first firing is not such a big deal.

But to go through the fire a second time is another matter altogether. Been there. Done that. Hated every minute of it. But sometimes that is exactly what we are called to do. Agree to the process. Go back. And do it again.

Going to an estranged brother again and again and again, risking the pain of rejection because there is some faint hope that reconciliation might be possible. And still persisting.

Going to the nursing home week after week after week to visit an ailing parent who is losing both awareness and ability as time goes by. And still persisting.

Going to a tiresome job day after day after day, even though it is not rewarding or fulfilling in any way. And still persisting.

Returning to a situation filled with pain and challenge is never easy.

Joseph's brothers knew it. When the famine was great in Israel, ten of Joseph's brothers went to Egypt to buy grain (Gen. 42). It was a long, dusty journey, and when they arrived, they had a strange and stressful interaction with Joseph who "pretended to be a stranger and spoke harshly to them" (42:7). Putting Egypt behind them, they returned to Israel and to their father

Jacob. But it wasn't long before their need became severe once more. Do they dare take another trip to Egypt? Yes, they do. And ultimately they are reunited with their brother.

Nehemiah knew it. When the walls of Jerusalem had fallen into disrepair, Nehemiah led a great initiative and rebuilt the walls and the gates of the great city (Neh. 1–6). More than forty-two thousand Hebrew exiles returned, and Jerusalem experienced a glorious rebirth (Neh. 7–12). His work complete, Nehemiah returned to Babylon, and while he was gone, things completely fell apart. Does he dare make another attempt to restore that city?

Yes, he does. And ultimately, he sees God's word triumph.

Moses knew it. When the Hebrews crossed the Red Sea into freedom, they needed God's guidance to give order to their lives. So God met with Moses on Mount Sinai:

> Mount Sinai was covered with smoke, because the Lord descended on it in fire. The smoke billowed up from it like smoke from a furnace, and the whole mountain trembled violently. As the sound of the trumpet grew louder and louder, Moses spoke and the voice of God answered him. (Exodus 19:18–19)

God wrote his law on stone tablets. Putting Sinai behind him, Moses walked back into camp. Seeing the golden calf, he was enraged and broke the tablets to pieces. Then God came to him a second time: "Chisel out two stone tablets like the first ones, and I will write on them the words that were on the first tablets" (Exod. 34:1). Does he dare face another meeting with the God of smoke and trembling? Yes, he does. And ultimately, the law of God is faithfully given.

For the clay pot, the first firing establishes its strength; the second time through the kiln brings out its color and full beauty. Transformed once and then again. In the words of 2 Corinthians 3:18, it represents a change from one degree of glory to the next.

Before the pot is fired the second time, it is glazed. Glaze is a suspension of finely ground minerals, mostly silica. As the temperature rises, the glaze melts, coating the pot in a glassy finish.

It takes courage, lots of courage, to submit and return, to go back and go through it again. Back to Egypt. Back to Jerusalem. Back to Mount Sinai. Back into the fire and flame. The second trip is infinitely harder than the first. But in the background is a whisper, a promise:

> The Lord is the everlasting God, the Creator of the ends of the earth. He will not grow tired or weary, and his understanding no one can fathom. He gives strength to the weary and increases the power of the weak. Even youths grow tired and weary, and young men stumble and fall; but those who hope in the Lord will renew their strength. They will soar on wings like eagles; they will run and not grow weary, they will walk and not be faint. (Isaiah 40:28–31)

REFLECTION & DISCUSSION

Is there some task that you have been afraid to face because you have been there before and it is too painful to imagine trying it again? Talk to God about it and ask for the courage to persist in doing what is right.

Is there some ongoing task that has become very nearly unbearable, but still you sense the need to stay and faithfully complete it? Ask God to transform the mundane into the miraculous so that you can see his hand even in the midst of this circumstance. And persist in trust, even when it's hard to see the purpose or impossible to imagine the outcome.

. . .

PRAYER

God, there are things in my life that are difficult
because I really have counted the cost and
experienced the pain and that makes it harder
for me to persevere. I pray that you will either
change my heart or change my circumstances.
And whichever it is that you choose to do,
I am determined to look for the ways that
love, joy, peace, patience, kindness, goodness,
faithfulness, gentleness, and self-control
will abound in my life. Amen.

STUDIO INSIGHTS

The second firing is called the glaze firing, and that is where the final transformation happens. The first firing changed the structure of the pot itself; the second transforms it.

Glazes come in a bewildering variety of colors and surface textures. In simple terms, glaze consists of three key components. *Silica* which is the primary glass-forming agent; *fluxes* that adjust the proper melting temperature; and *alumina,* which acts a stabilizer. Oxides are added to this base to achieve various colors, and additional chemicals may be added to the mix in order to create texture, change the color, or modify the finish. The result is a thick liquid suspension.

Once bisque-fired pots are cooled and removed from the kiln, potters apply the glaze. They may dip the pots into large buckets of glaze, or brush it on or spray it.

Before firing, the colors of the glaze appear dry, dusty, muted, and pale, but under the heat of the firing process, they are transformed into something greater than the sum of their parts. Powder becomes glass, and vibrant color is revealed. Although experienced potters can be relatively sure how the glazed pots will come out, there are always surprises. This makes kiln openings exciting each and every time.

REDEEMING

IF THE FINISHED POT
IS DROPPED AND SHATTERED,
GOD IS NOT DAUNTED.

There it sits, bright and beautiful: a vase on the dining room table holding fresh flowers, or the mug on your desk holding morning coffee. Our pot is finished.

So let's imagine the unimaginable.

What happens if this strong, colorful, beautiful, finished pot is dropped? Even now, even at this point in the process, it is still possible for the potter to redeem it.

Several years ago, I began experimenting with a new art form: mosaic. I had seen examples of mosaics, small and large, and was attracted to the beauty and potential of this process.

A restaurant not far from my house has an exquisite entryway made entirely of large, richly colored pieces of broken pottery, arranged in a bright, bold abstract design. A fountain in a neighborhood courtyard is covered with very small pieces of colorful ceramic tiles.

I have seen ancient mosaics in museums, some of them more than twelve feet high, and they contain complex images of people, horses, battles, columns, and other stirring scenes. After thousands of years, the colors are still astonishingly bright, clear, strong, and beautiful.

Even the ceramic tiles that you might find on your bathroom wall, your kitchen counter, or the floor of your front hall are a kind of mosaic, beautiful, durable surfaces that are constructed out of smaller pieces of glazed and fired clay.

Those large, ancient mosaics in the museum and the bright, modern trim in the restaurant are made through very similar processes. A clean, smooth surface is prepared, and the small pieces of glazed and fired clay are glued into place. Then grout is applied over the entire thing. Grout looks and feels a lot like cake frosting. It is worked into all of the cracks in between the pieces and then smoothed out.

Then the surface of each clay piece is carefully wiped clean with a damp sponge. After the grout hardens, in a few hours or a day or two, the clay tiles are buffed with a soft cloth to remove every trace of grout from their surface.

I usually use broken dishes when I make mosaics. I take broken teacups and dinner plates and soup bowls and combine the small pieces in new ways to decorate a birdhouse, flowerpot, or tabletop. As I work, I am reminded of the miracle of redemption. I have a friend who is a quilter. She uses bits of fabric in much the same way as I use bits of clay, joining old scraps together in new ways, making something of beauty and great worth.

The original ceramic piece served one purpose, and it was good in its season. The brand-new composite piece will serve its purpose, too. And it is good in its season.

It is interesting to me that when my students and my friends found out that I was making mosaics, they started to bring me chipped bowls, split plates, cracked statuary, and broken coffee mugs. Every now and then I would arrive at work in the morning to find a grocery bag filled with old pottery sitting in front of my office door! There have been serving platters in my mailbox, porcelain birds on my desk, and sacks of old, unmatched saucers on my rocking chair.

One dear friend has taken to prowling estate sales and flea markets searching for chipped china that I can repurpose. Another friend used the opportunity to buy herself a whole new set of dishes and give me her old place settings! Each piece, broken into chunks and combined with other shards and cast-offs, has become the raw material for something brand new.

It is especially interesting to me to hear my friends say that knowing about this art form has really changed their perspective. Before, when a dish was dropped or a cup got chipped, they would spit and fume. So frustrating! What a disaster! Now, when pottery pieces get broken, they smile: "Wow, look at that. I wonder what Diana can make out of this one?"

They see the accident as an opportunity to make a contribution to an artistic cause. It's interesting, isn't it, that the situation didn't change. Just their point of view.

Rightly understood, there is no raw material, no accident, no broken pieces that our Creator God can't redeem. Because no matter what, God is never, ever, ever daunted.

REFLECTION & DISCUSSION

List several situations where you have told yourself, "It's too late." Then offer the list to God in prayer.

Take time this week to appreciate the beauty of a mosaic, a quilt, a collage, a scrapbook page, or another art form that is made when an artist redeems bits and pieces by making something brand new. Or set aside time to exercise your own creative gifts in this way.

· · ·

PRAYER

Change my heart, O God, so that I may learn
to be always alert to the redemptive opportunities
that can be found in even the sorriest mess. Amen.

STUDIO INSIGHTS

There are a number of ways that broken pottery pieces can be redeemed, and one of the most remarkable is the ancient Japanese technique called *kintsugi*. The word "kintsugi" means to join using gold.

The process begins by skillfully, patiently connecting the broken shards using urushi lacquer, a rare substance derived from tree sap. The thick lacquer forms a very strong bond. It is left to dry and then sanded smooth.

Next, the pot is dusted with 24k gold powder. Other precious metals are sometimes used, such as silver, copper, or platinum. The metal adheres to the lacquer and highlights each crack in a visible, tangible way.

When traditional materials are used, the process is quite labor-intensive and requires a great deal of patience. It can take several days for each piece to dry as the shards are being carefully connected. But when the kintsugi process is complete, the pot will be much more valuable than it was before it was damaged. The newly mended piece will also stand as a testimony to the beauty that lies hidden all around us.

The practice of kintsugi is closely tied to the philosophy of wabi-sabi, which encourages acceptance of the impermanence of this world. It expresses delight in imperfection and celebrates the beauty that can be found in brokenness. It redeems cracks, breaks, chips, and flaws by emphasizing and enhancing them, not by ignoring them or denying them or hiding them away.

Kintsugi represents an attitude of tender care toward fragile things. Rather than throwing things away and continuing to acquire more and more, we care for the earth and each other by cultivating the practice of reclaiming and restoring. And redeeming.

A B I D I N G

WE LEARN TO RECOGNIZE
GOD'S EXTRAORDINARY WORK
IN THE MIDST OF OUR ORDINARY,
EVERYDAY LIVES.

It has been a long journey from the stillness of the mountainside, where thick deposits of clay were hidden, to the joy of the one who found the clay and carried it home, to the patient process of cleaning, wedging, attaching, opening, and shaping the clay, to the flash of fire and the final transformation brought about by intensity and perseverance. We have seen how things look when all goes well. We have also seen that our sovereign God is not daunted by those events we think of as mistakes, missteps, sidetracks, and accidents. All these things work together for good!

We are so much like that clay, loved by the Great Artist, brought into his household, and shaped as he sees fit. Looking back, we realize that somehow

God has been able to use us in the work he is doing in this world. We remain, as Paul says, "joyful in hope, patient in affliction, faithful in prayer" (Rom. 12:12). It is true that times get hard, yet there is hope and purpose:

> We are hard pressed on every side, but not crushed; perplexed, but not in despair; persecuted, but not abandoned; struck down, but not destroyed. (2 Corinthians 4:8–9)

How is it possible that we live in such hope? Because we know that we are earthen vessels, jars of clay, carrying around the life of Jesus in us as a testimony that the all-surpassing power is from God and definitely not from us (2 Cor. 4:7).

There are so many ways in which we resemble that clay pot and reflect the process that it has been through under the potter's loving hand. But there are important differences, too. The pot goes through the steps of the process just this once. Then it is finished. It is strong and beautiful, ready for the Master's use.

On the other hand, we are living vessels. We find ourselves circling back and repeating various stages of the process. Oh, we may be revisiting a stage in the process but at a higher level. Throughout our lives, we find that God still has just a bit more work to do. He needs to reshape and refine us afresh, until that great day when we are like Christ, when we see him face-to-face (1 John 3:2).

WHERE ARE YOU TODAY
IN THIS ONGOING PROCESS?

Feeling a little lost, off the beaten path? Feeling alone, wondering, watching, waiting, but not yet responsive to God's call?

Being cleaned and prepared, separated from worldliness, feeling the debris being pulled from your life, hating the loss on the one hand, welcoming the cleansing touch that brings freedom on the other?

Getting wedged—pushed and pushed and pushed again—so that each and every part of your life is aligned, marked by complete integrity?

Challenged to make a commitment, no longer allowed to wiggle and waffle, invited to say a decisive *yes* to God's process?

Centering, letting go of the extraneous things that knock you off course, fine-tuning your focus, bringing your will into complete agreement with God's will, finding God's *Shalom*?

Opening up, letting go, creating space, allowing times of solitude and silence so that God can speak the truth deep into your soul?

Getting grounded, stable, steady, establishing the details of your daily life on a firm foundation?

Pulled and shaped, dealing with pressure that is helping you grow in surprising, even miraculous ways?

Waiting, feeling dry, getting impatient, wondering when it will be time for your breakthrough?

Surprised by the fire, the intensity, the heat, the challenge, the pain, the disappointment?

Frightened by the prospect of a second, third, or fourth time back into that same hardship that was almost unbearable the last time through?

Humbled by how tenderly God has gathered disappointments and broken hopes and dreams and shaped them into beauty and grace you could not have imagined?

Abiding, confident in faith that our loving, creative God abides with us.

Unlike the human potter, the Divine Potter is never finished. In his infinite creativity, God is always at work, drawing near, bringing about something new.

And in the midst of our ordinary everyday lives, we become more and more aware of the way he is working and increasingly able to cooperate with the process. It gets easier to experience God's presence in good times and in difficult ones. We learn to look for the signs that God is at work and learn to recognize the kind of work that he is doing. We discover new depths of God's wisdom and grace. We deepen in faith and grow in trust, believing that our Creator and Redeemer is making something beautiful of our lives.

REFLECTION & DISCUSSION

Which step in the process do you relate to in this season of your life? Ask God to help you become more aware of his comfort, provision, and purpose, even now. Are there steps that you have been deliberately resisting, avoiding, or neglecting? Ask God to make you willing to be made willing to surrender to that step in the process.

. . .

PRAYER

God, I am fearfully and wonderfully made. You called me into being and have shaped me by your hand. Through times of long dryness, times of intense fire, and times of immeasurable blessing—you have been with me. Now, help me to recognize the ways you are at work in the midst of my current circumstances. Teach me to see the evidence of your extraordinary work in my life. Give me the wisdom and the courage to cooperate with you in the process. Let me abide in your life-giving presence today and every day and throughout all the seasons of my life. Amen.

STUDIO INSIGHTS

Each pot is unique, and each one has been in the hands of the potter every step of the way. Some potters find it tough to see finished pots leave the studio. They note a feeling of loss when pieces are purchased or given away. That closeness, those feelings of connection and lasting affection, stand as a witness to the kind of love our Creator feels for his creation.

In truth, each pot is made for a purpose, and that purpose is not to sit on a shelf in my studio. It moves out of these close confines and into homes and churches, galleries and schools, kitchens and gardens. It may bring beauty, joy, and pleasure in each new setting. Or it may inspire new creativity, energy, challenge, vision, and meaning. Perhaps it adorns a table, holds a cup of morning coffee, or serves up fresh baked bread. Decorative or functional, each piece of handmade pottery fulfills a unique purpose. Fearfully and wonderfully made, it finds its purpose as it brings something of worth to this world.

RECOMMENDED READING

Bentz, Joseph. *When God Takes Too Long.*
This book gives real help in understanding why things take so long and
what we can do to stay hopeful and productive in the meantime.

Carter, Ben. *Mastering the Potter's Wheel.*
This manual for potters offers wonderful detail on all aspects of working
with clay. It is clear, comprehensive, and very well-written.

Foster, Richard. *Celebration of Discipline* and *Freedom of Simplicity.*
There are several books that I make a point of re-reading regularly, and
these two are especially meaningful for me. Meaningful and humbling—
I am always convicted by what Foster has to say.

Fujimura, Makoto. *Art and Faith.* Yale University Press, 2020.
The fruit of over thirty years of painting and creating in his studio, this
book is Fujimura's exploration of creativity and the spiritual aspects of
"making." Mako also appears in several Square Halo titles, including
It Was Good and *Objects of Grace.*

Keller, W. Phillip. *A Shepherd Looks at Psalm 23.*
One of the most beautiful word pictures God gives us to describe
himself is that of a shepherd watching over his sheep. Keller worked as a
shepherd, and so when he reads the twenty-third psalm, he understands
the fullness of its meaning. A comforting, encouraging classic.

Lewis, C.S. *The Problem of Pain* and *A Grief Observed.*
Sometimes we need help to understand why so many bad things happen
and why God sometimes seems distant and unfair. Sometimes, we need
to know that other people have gone through times of personal hardship
and understand how we feel. Lewis has written both kinds of books:
The Problem of Pain is an intellectual answer to the question of evil;
A Grief Observed is the diary he kept when his wife, Joy Davidman, died.
Each book is splendid in its own way.

Packer, J.I. *Knowing God.*
A classic exploration of God's nature and character. Read it to get better
acquainted with the God who loves you.

Roach, Steven and Ned Bustard. *Naming the Animals.*
This book asserts that all of us were made in the image of an imaginative
God, and in that light encourages us to see creativity as an essential part of
God's design for partnership with humanity. This book is the best place to
begin when seeking to learn about the relationship between Faith and Art.

Sayers, Dorothy L. *The Mind of the Maker.*
Sayers takes a thoughtful look at the nature of creativity and how
God's creativity is reflected in us.

Willard, Dallas. *The Spirit of the Disciplines.*
Substantial and thought-provoking, this book helps us understand how
the spiritual disciplines become tools of transformation in our lives.

ACKNOWLEDGMENTS

We owe a great debt of thanks to many people who have encouraged and supported us, not only in this project but also in the ongoing process of recognizing and cooperating with the hand of God in our daily lives. In preparing this Square Halo edition, we owe a special debt of gratitude to our friends at The Rabbit Room. The vision for this project took shape at Hutchmoot. We would also like to acknowledge the faithful collaboration of these dear friends:

The Niños, creative artists who continue to persevere in prayer; the departments of Art and Design at APU (especially Bill, Sue, Tom, Guy, and Terry); Annie and Matthew who prayed, encouraged, and taught me much in the process; Lynn Maudlin, who came to the rescue; Barbara Hayes who proofread and gave wonderful advice; and Adam Bradley, my colleague and friend. This book would not exist without you.
—*Diana*

My exceedingly patient wife, Ellie, who encouraged and supported this project even as we awaited and welcomed our daughter, May Hương; My brother Tài San, for helping capture the photos while I was covered in clay; Ted and Cathy Prescott for years of support, mentorship, and many, many, prayers.
—*Quay*

My pottery students (past, present, and future)—you helped refine my knowledge of clay as we created together, and your energy, creativity, and encouragement kept my love for clay going when I was in the fire. Betty Copeland, for viewing me as a *potter* who teaches before I could ever hope of seeing that for myself.
—*Eddy*

AUTHORS AND ARTISTS

DIANA PAVLAC GLYER is a potter, painter, and avid gardener. She teaches in the Honors College at Azusa Pacific University. She enjoys the work of C.S. Lewis and J.R.R. Tolkien and has published books and articles about their creative process. She lives in southern California. To learn more, visit www.DianaGlyer.com

QUAY SAN is a potter, photographer, and pastor, living in Camp Hill, Pennsylvania. He serves full-time as the Junior High Pastor at West Shore Free Church in Mechanicsburg, Pennsylvania, and makes pots out of his home studio. He's interested in art as the product of a maker's life—lived faithfully and productively—and the value of beauty for the body of Christ and the world around us. His work is influenced by the shapes and sensibilities of his mixed Vietnamese upbringing and the wonders of glaze chemistry. You can find his work at www.QuaySan.art

EDDY EFAW is a native of West Virginia, and it was here that he fell in love with clay at Fairmont State College. Having taught ceramics and visual arts at Harding Academy of Memphis for over twenty-five years, what he enjoys most about ceramics is the opportunity it offers to bring beauty into the lives of others. You can find out more about his work at www.EddyEfaw.com

GLOSSARY

BANDING WHEEL a turntable used to place pottery upon to trim the rim or add decorative images, patterns, or lines

BAT a plastic, wooden, or plaster disc that is affixed to the wheel head before throwing

BISQUE FIRE an initial firing that removes all physical and chemical water and turns clay into ceramic, which will no longer dissolve in water. This leaves the piece highly porous and ready to be glazed.

BONE DRY the condition of clay when all of the moisture is gone. This is the most fragile condition for a clay body.

BURNISHING polishing leather-hard clay with a hard object to give it a smooth, hard finish

CENTERING making a lump of clay perfectly symmetrical in all directions on the potter's wheel

CHAMOIS a small piece of leather that can be dipped in water and gently placed on the lip of a pot while it is spinning on the wheel to make the rim smooth and strong

CLAY a decomposed granite-type rock. To be classified as clay, the rock must have fine particles so that it will be plastic/pliable.

CLAY BODY a mixture of clay and sometimes other minerals that are blended for various ceramic purposes

COLLARING gently coaxing clay inward with both hands while the wheel is spinning. The neck of a vase or bottles is made by collaring.

COMPOSITE POT a piece that is made up of various parts. A teapot is a composite of a lidded jar, handle, and spout.

CONING pushing clay inward and upward into a cone shape, where it can more easily be coaxed into center, usually the first step in centering and repeated multiple times

CROSS-SECTION created by making a straight cut through a piece of pottery from bottom to top. This type of cut allows a potter to see the width of the walls and base of their throw piece.

CYLINDER an open form with straight, parallel sides and a circular cross-section

DAMP BOX a plastic, lidded container with 1–2 inches of damp plaster in the bottom. used to keep pots leather-hard

EARTHENWARE a low-fired clay body (1,650–1,940°F) clay body, usually white, buff, or red-orange

EMBOSS carve, mold, or stamp a design on the surface of a pot so that it stands out in relief.

ENGRAVE to cut or carve (a text or design) on the surface of a hard object

ETCH to create a pattern or design on a leather-hard or bone-dry pot by scratching the surface of the piece

FETTLING KNIFE a sharp instrument with a flexible blade tapering to a point. Used in ceramics for carving, sgraffito, and shaping clay.

FIRING heating ceramic ware in a kiln to create a chemical change in the clay to make it permanently hard

FLUX a substance used to lower the melting point of the glass-forming components of glazes and ceramic bodies

FOOT the bottom or base of a ceramic piece

GLAZE finely ground minerals in a liquid form that are applied to the surface of bisque-fired pottery

GLAZE FIRE a firing cycle that heats pottery to the temperature at which the glaze materials will melt to create a glass-like coating on the surface of a piece of pottery.

GREENWARE a clay object that has not been fired yet

GROG a sand-like material made of fired clay. It is added to plastic clay to increase its strength and workability.

GROUT mortar or paste used for filling crevices between tiles or broken ceramic material in a mosaic

HEATWORK the combined effect of temperature and time applied to clay during firing in a kiln

HIGH FIRE stoneware or porcelain clay fired to a temperature between 2,012–2,336°F (1,100–1,280°C). Cones 07–10 are high fire cones.

HYDROPLANING adding water to the wheel head so that after wiring a pot off from the wheel, it can be slid onto a board.

KICK WHEEL a potter's wheel worked by a foot pedal or by kicking a heavy disk at the foot of the vertical shaft. These wheels allow potters to work without the need for electricity.

KIDNEY a tool made of steel, rubber, or wood that is used to smooth and shape pots as they are shaped on the potter's wheel.

KILN a furnace made of refractory clay materials for firing ceramic products

KINTSUGI the Japanese art of repairing broken pottery by mending broken areas with urushi lacquer and then dusting the lines with gold powder

LEATHER-HARD the condition of a clay body when some of the moisture has left the clay body but it is still soft enough to be carved or cut easily.

LIP the top edge of a mug, bowl, or vase

LOOP TOOL a tool made from a loop of wire attached to a wooden or plastic handle. This wire can vary in thickness and be bent into an endless variety of shapes. Loop tools are typically used for removing clay during decorating and sculpting but can also be used as trimming tools on the wheel.

LOW FIRE a clay body that is fired at a relatively low temperature, typically between 1,650–2,000°F. Cones 04–06 are low fire cones.

MAKER'S MARK a signature or logo that is stamped or scratched into a vessel to identify the one who made it.

NEEDLE TOOL a long metal needle set into a wooden, metal, or plastic handle. It is used for cutting, piercing, incising, measuring depth, scoring, and finishing fine details.

OPAQUE not transparent or translucent, not able to be seen through

OXIDE raw pigments from which glazes and stains are created. Oxides may be used as stains.

PLASTIC the condition of clay when it is moist and easy to mold and manipulate into any desired form

PLASTICITY clay's ability to be shaped without breaking and then retain that form

PORCELAIN a fine-textured, light colored, delicate clay

PUGMILL a machine used to mix large quantities of unfired clay into a homogeneous mixture suitable for the potter's use

PULLING lifting the walls of an open form by adding pressure on the inside and outside and slowly raising the hands up as the wheel is spinning

PYROMETRIC CONES small triangular cones (.125 x 1 inch) made of ceramic materials that are made to bend and melt at specific temperatures, thus enabling the potter to know when the firing is finished

RAM'S HEAD WEDGING kneading and rolling clay onto the table with your hands with equal pressure. As it progresses, the clay will begin to look like a ram's head.

RIB a wooden, metal, or plastic tool that is used to shape pots; it is called a rib because at one time potters used the rib bones of animals for this purpose.

SCORING a technique of cutting small lines into the surface of a clay body in a cross-hatching pattern

S-CRACK a crack in the base of a pot that looks similar to an elongated "S"; such cracks develop when the base and walls of the pot have different rates of shrinkage in the drying stage.

SGRAFFITO a technique where potters can put a layer of glaze or slip on a piece of pottery, let it dry, then use a pottery carving tool to scratch through to show the base layer of color. Sgraffito derives from an Italian word meaning "to scratch."

SHARD a broken piece of pottery

SHRINKAGE Clay shrinks in drying as water leaves the ware. Clay also gets smaller during firing when the vitrification process occurs. Rates can be as little as 4% or as much as 15% for some clay bodies.

SIEVE fixed screens that wet or dry materials are pushed through to remove larger than desired particles; the higher the mesh number, the finer the screen.

SINTERING (FRITTAGE) the process of forming a solid mass of material through heat and pressure without melting to the point of liquefaction

SLAB a piece of clay typically flattened by a rolling pin or dowel rod for use in hand-building.

SLAKING how a dry clay disintegrates when it is immersed in or exposed to water. Different clays have different slaking rates.

SLIP a liquid form of clay that can be used to decorate the surface of clay or to join two pieces of clay together

SLIP TRAILING applying lines of slip to a clay surface using a fine-pointed dispenser. Slips are generally applied to leather-hard work, even though some can be applied to bone dry or even bisqueware.

SLURRY thick, liquid clay (sometimes inconsistent in texture) used to glue or join clay pieces together before firing. Slip is much smoother and is poured into molds to make perfect, smooth copies of the shape.

SPIRAL WEDGING using a rocking motion with your hands, gripping the clay at the top, and pressing the clay down a little to the left in a repetitive motion causing the clay to have a spiral design

SPRIGGING a low-relief clay attachment that is applied to pottery before firing; created by carving or pressing designs into plaster or clay then pressing the final clay into the clay mold before removing and attaching to the pot

STONEWARE a high-fired clay body (2,200–2,350°F); much stronger than earthenware; functional use

TERRA COTTA red-orange earthenware

THERMAL SHOCK occurs when changes in temperature occur in the kiln during heating and cooling; it can happen outside the kiln as well such as when a pot is placed in the microwave or dishwasher.

THROWING a method of forming pottery vessels on a potter's wheel

TORQUE the true measure of a pottery wheel's power. Larger motors on electric wheels will create more power, adding pressure to clay moving on a potter's wheel in order to center it

TRIMMING carving away excess clay from the foot or sides of a pot using sharp metal tools while the wheel is spinning

TURNING the process of finishing leather-hard ware using tools to cut off small "shavings" of clay in order to smooth and finish the sides, or to

establish foot rings and bases for pots. Turning is usually done on the potter's wheel as the piece spins.

UNDERGLAZE glaze that can be painted on a piece at the leather-hard or bisque ware stage; it will be seen as a matte finish unless a clear glaze is placed over it after it dries

VITRIFICATION a process where the clay is physically and chemically changed by firing it in a kiln. This makes the ware impervious to water.

WALL the continuous, vertical side of a pot; potters "lift" the walls of a piece while the clay is spinning on a potter's wheel

WARE a group of ceramic products based on the specific type of clay body used to create it (stoneware, earthenware, and agateware are all examples)

WARP when pieces twist and become uneven or asymmetrical during the drying process

WAX RESIST a type of glaze decoration that involves the application of a coat of one glaze, then painting a wax pattern, then applying a second coat of the same or a different glaze. The wax resists the second glaze from adhering, allowing the painted design to show through after it is fired.

WEDGING kneading clay in order to obtain a uniform texture that is free from air pockets

WHEEL HEAD the heavy, circular, metal piece that sits atop the shaft and motor of a potter's wheel

WHEEL THROWN pots that are made on a potter's wheel

WIRE CUTTER a tool used by potters to cut their finished pieces from the wheel or bat. Wire cutters are made by affixing a thin wire between two small pieces of wood or plastic.

MORE BOOKS ABOUT
CREATIVITY & FAITH

NAMING THE ANIMALS: AN INVITATION TO CREATIVITY

Drawing upon the biblical account of Creation and the witness of a myriad of creative thinkers, this book asserts that all of us were made in the image of an imaginative God. *Naming the Animals* encourages us to see creativity as an essential part of God's design for partnership with humanity.

IT WAS GOOD: MAKING ART TO THE GLORY OF GOD

What does it mean to be a creative individual who is a follower of the creative God? The *It Was Good* Series seeks to answer that question through collections of essays which offer theoretical and practical insights into artmaking from a Christian perspective. This first book in the series addresses all of the arts with an emphasis in the visual arts.

LIFTING THE VEIL: IMAGINATION AND THE KINGDOM OF GOD

From the moment that Jesus Christ first proclaimed the Kingdom of God, he appealed to our imagination. In this book, the poet Malcolm Guite explores how the creative work of poets and other artists can begin to lift the veil, kindling our imaginations for Christ.

WHY WE CREATE: REFLECTIONS ON THE CREATOR, THE CREATION, AND CREATING

What is the relationship between the Creator and His subcreators? What does it mean to be created "in the image of God"? How can I use my talents to the glory of God? and Why do humans create at all?

SQUAREHALOBOOKS.COM